D1148607

IDENTIFICATION GUIDES

British & European Trees

TONBRIDGE SCHOOL LIBRARY

R73251W0502

Publisher and Creative Director: Nick Wells
Project Editor: Sara Robson
Picture Research: Gemma Walters
Consultant Naturalist: Chris McLaren
Art Director: Mike Spender
Digital Design and Production: Chris Herbert
Layout Design: Basil UK Ltd.

Special thanks to: Chelsea Edwards, Julie Pallot, Sarah Sherman, Helen Tovey and Claire Walker

11 10

3 5 7 9 10 8 6 4 2

This edition first published 2007 by
FLAME TREE PUBLISHING
Crabtree Hall, Crabtree Lane
Fulham, London SW6 6TY
United Kingdom

www.flametreepublishing.com

Flame Tree Publishing is part of the Foundry Creative Media Co. Ltd.
© 2007 text and artwork illustrations Malcolm Saunders Publishing Ltd.
This edition produced under a licence granted by Malcolm Saunders Publishing Ltd.

© 2007 this edition The Foundry Creative Media Co. Ltd.

ISBN 978-1-84451-855-5

A CIP record for this book is available from the British Library upon request.

All rights reserved. No part of this publication may be reproduced, stored in a retrieval system,
or transmitted in any form or by any means, electronic, mechanical, photocopying,
recording or otherwise, without the prior permission in writing of the publisher.

All photographs courtesy of Corbis, except p.98–9 courtesy of NHPA/Photoshot: R. Sorensen and J. Olsen.

Printed in China

582.16
A752S1W

IDENTIFICATION GUIDES

British & European Trees

Pamela Forey

FLAME TREE
PUBLISHING

Contents

Introduction

The chief aim of this book is to enable the reader to identify positively and as simply as possible the great majority of European trees which he is likely to encounter.

A great number of people may not have the time or the opportunity to develop a detailed interest in trees but would appreciate some means by which they can easily identify a tree that may attract their attention, on holiday, for instance, or on a country walk, or simply one that catches the eye in a local park or garden.

Faced with tree books which contain the entire list of European trees, most people are quite bemused. Where do you start looking if, as is almost invariably the case, the trees are systematically grouped in families. The beginner, understandably, probably has little or no idea into which family a particular tree falls. So this book is arranged in a different way. The trees are grouped according to their leaf shapes, an easily recognizable feature.

The trees are all described and illustrated in their spring and autumn forms with autumn fruits, since it is at these times that the new observer is likely to be attracted by them. Emphasis is given to flowers and fruits, as well as to leaves, since, as well as being the most obvious, they are also the most characteristic and easily identifiable features of the tree.

Finally, this book does not claim to present a complete list with its 'featured trees' (those with an entire spread including a full colour plate). In such a large area as Europe, there is wide variation in the species found from north to south. So trees that are rare or absent in the north may be common or even dominant in the south, and vice versa. Some native trees have been omitted if they grow in remote areas where people seldom go or if they have limited distributions; other introduced or hybrid species have been included because they are commonly planted in streets or parks or gardens where the non-expert is likely to notice them and wonder what they are.

How to Use this Book

This book is divided into three basic sections, **Broad-Leaved Trees**, **Palms and Palm-Like Trees** and **Conifers**. A fourth section, **Lookalikes and Cultivars**, complements the first three.

Using the **Guide to Identification** to tree and leaf type (see p.12), first decide to which of the above sections your tree belongs. The leaf symbols will help you to narrow down the field and the information contained on the left-hand page beside the illustration of each tree makes a positive identification possible and eliminates confusion. A specimen spread is shown in Fig. 1 (see p.11).

Primary Features

Where feasible, the reader will be able to recognize the tree from the primary characteristics described in the first paragraph, under **Primary Features**, together with the illustration. However, sometimes it is a combination of features that identifies a tree, firstly as a type of tree (e.g. as an oak, if it has acorns) and then as a particular species (e.g. as a Common Oak if it has stalked acorns). The reader can be sure that he has identified the tree when it has all the characteristics of the **Primary Features** and **Secondary Features**.

However, trees present a time problem in that, for example, if the **Primary Features** identifies the tree by its flowers, then this paragraph can only be used at certain times of the year. The **Secondary Features** paragraph therefore includes complementary data on fruits and leaves which enables the reader to identify the tree at other times of the year.

Flowers and Fruits

You will also find flowering and fruiting times at the foot of the page, but it is important to realise that these are guides only. A tree growing in southern Europe will come into flower many weeks earlier than one of the same species growing in northern areas. Flowering times are probably more reliable guides on the whole than fruiting times, which tend to be much more variable. The fruiting times usually refer to ripe fruit – it is worth remembering that if a tree flowers in spring or early summer and the fruiting time given is in the autumn, then the fruits will be visible throughout the summer, gradually growing and developing until they ripen. Therefore, fruits will often be present on a tree for much longer periods of time than the flowers and if allowance is made for immaturity of size and colour, then they can be used to help you in identification.

The third paragraph, under **Localities and Habits**, is a general guide to the distribution of the trees in Europe (Britain is classified as being in northern or western Europe), and it also gives environmental details, including soil preferences, trees that grow in cities, beside water and so on.

Avoiding Confusion

The fourth paragraph on each spread, under **Lookalikes**, gives the names of similar trees with which the featured tree could be confused. All these 'lookalikes' are either featured in detail themselves or, if contained in brackets, appear under the heading of **Lookalikes and Cultivars** in the last section. The 'lookalikes' paragraph is important for two reasons. Firstly, it is always possible to jump to conclusions when looking for known identifying features. You can in effect already have made up your mind on a tree's identity before checking out the primary points. Some species of trees resemble each other quite closely. Secondly, it is very important for the reader to become aware of exactly which groups of trees resemble each other so that he can check out the differences. This is where the guesswork ends and the skill begins.

The **Lookalikes and Cultivars** section consists of 1) a group of less common species for which the featured trees may be mistaken; 2) a selection of common garden varieties of a few trees, including Japanese Cherries, Magnolias, Hollies and Eucalypts, all of which have so many varieties that they could not be given space enough in the featured trees sections; and 3) the commoner varieties of conifers, so popular as hedging and specimen trees in modern gardens.

Check Your Sightings

So now we come to it. At last you can identify the tree on the corner where you sheltered from the rain, or the one in the next road that has such lovely blossom every year. But remember that trees grow very slowly, so treat the size indication with caution! Just because we have said that this is a large tree does not mean that you have identified it wrongly if it is small – it may be just young. But the leaves, flowers and fruits will not change for they are characteristic of that species of tree. Now you know how to use this book. You are equipped with all the knowledge you need for the moment.

Good luck – and don't forget to tick off your sightings on the checklist provided with the index!

Specimen Spread

Deciduous or evergreen

Relative size

Symbol of leaf type: see Guide to Identification

Colour illustration of characteristics

FIG. 1

Name of tree

Colour denotes type of tree

130

Hornbeam

Deciduous, Medium

Primary Features

Fruiting spike consists of about eight pairs of small nuts, each one cupped in a three-lobed bract at first green later brown, the whole making a loose bunch.

Secondary Features

A medium sized tree in which the twigs grow horizontally in a zig zag pattern. Male catkins up to 5 cm long, greenish yellow, drooping. Female catkins about 2 cm long, green, drooping.

Localities and Habits

Hedgerows, woods, sometimes coppiced, sometimes planted as a street tree. Over much of Europe.

Lookalikes

Hop Hornbeam p.134, Beech p.142

Flowering and Fruiting Periods

Flowers April–May, fruit July–October

131

♂ male

♀ female

Colour photograph offering an alternative view of the tree.

Guide to Identification

Broad-Leaved Trees

Trees with a host of small, thin, broad leaves growing on woody branches which spread from one or several woody stems or trunks. These trees bear flowers at certain times of the year (some with petals like the Rowan or the Orange Tree; others with fluffy clusters of petal-less flowers like Ash or Elm; others with catkins like Willow or Oak) and most bear dry or juicy fruits. If your tree fits this description, then consult the following sub-sections:

Trees with simple leaves

In these trees the leaves are entire and undivided and not lobed in any way. Very many trees have leaves of this type and so, to enable you to find your tree more quickly, we have divided the sub-section into three groups:

Simple leaves with single teeth

In these trees the leaves have edges which may bear sharp or rounded, fine or coarse teeth. If the leaves of your tree are so finely toothed that you are unsure of their placement, or if some are toothed and some are not, then you should look in the section on trees with simple leaves without teeth as well.

This is quite a large group and the trees are arranged so that those having leaves with teeth are at the beginning of the group and those having leaves with coarser teeth are at the end; a quick comparison will show you whether it would be better for you to start at the beginning of the group and work forwards or at the end and work backwards.

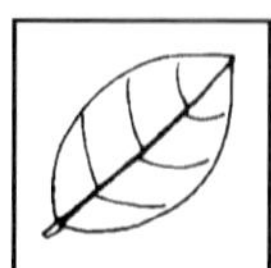

Simple leaves with double teeth

In these trees the leaves have quite coarsely toothed edges in which the coarse teeth are also toothed – hence double teeth.

Simple leaves without teeth

In these trees the edges of the leaves are generally toothless. However, some of the leaves may have a few irregular teeth or the edges may be so finely toothed that it is really quite difficult to decide whether they are toothed or not. If in doubt, then you should check the beginning of the group of trees with simple leaves and single teeth as well. Some of the leaves in this group have edges that are wavy (see Beech p.142) or spiny or both. Spines are not the same as teeth (see Holly p.174, for example).

Trees with lobed leaves

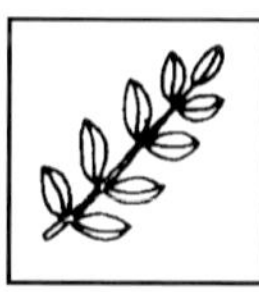

In these trees the blades of the leaves are divided into lobes, either pairs of lobes, as in the Common Oak diagram left, or into more triangular lobes, as in the Sycamore (p.214). In none of these leaves do the lobes extend to the base of the leaf or to the central line of the leaf, to divide it into separate leaflets. If you have a leaf which is split right to the base or to the central line, then you should look at the next section, on trees with compound leaves.

Trees with compound leaves

The blades of these leaves are divided into either a few or many separate leaflets, usually along the length of the leaf as in the Rowan diagram on the left, but sometimes the leaflets all grow from one point at the top of the leaf-stalk as in the Horse Chestnut (p.244).

Palms and Palm-Like Trees

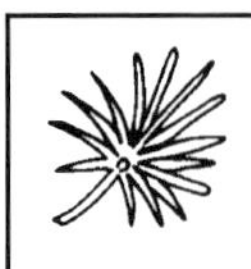

Trees in which the trunks are formed from old leaf-bases; they are not real, woody trunks at all. The leaves grow in a dense crown from the tops of the trunks and may be simple, fan-shaped or finely divided compound leaves. If your tree fits this description, then you can turn directly to the featured plants of this section.

Conifers

Trees with a regular appearance and very many small, either needle-like or scale-like leaves growing from woody branches spreading from a single woody trunk. These trees bear small separate male and female 'flowers' like miniature cones. The female flowers develop into mature cones which contain the seeds, or in a few species, into seed-bearing 'berries'. If your tree fits this description, then consult the following sub-sections:

Trees with needle-like leaves

In these trees the leaves are like needles. They may grow in rows or spirals along the branches, or they may grow in clusters (see Cedar of Lebanon, p.296) or in pairs (see Scots Pine, p.304).

Trees with scale-like leaves

In these trees the leaves are small and scale-like and clothe the branches so closely that the branches often look green and feathery. In a few trees the scale-like leaves are spiky as in the Chinese Juniper (p.312).

Glossary of Terms

Axil The more-or-less V-shaped angle made by the junction between a leaf and a stem or twig.

Boss A rough area on a trunk where many shoots grow.

Bract A green leafy structure which has a flower in its axil, and which may remain on the plant with the fruit. Bracts vary enormously in size, shape and function.

Capsule A dry fruit which splits open to release the seeds.

Catkin A drooping spike of small flowers. Male catkins produce the pollen; the female catkins are pollinated and then develop into fruiting catkins which bear the seeds.

Cone The flowers and fruit of a conifer – a cone-bearing tree. Male cones produce pollen; female cones produce the seeds. The mature brownish, woody seed-bearing cones are the most conspicuous and may be large and conical or small and conical.

Deciduous A deciduous tree is one which loses its leaves in winter.

Evergreen An evergreen tree is one which bears leaves throughout the year.

Fruits These contain the seeds. They may be dry or juicy, brown or brightly coloured, prickly or smooth etc.

Garden escape A cultivated garden plant which is growing in the wild.

Hybrid A plant which has originated from crossing one species of plant with another. Hybrids may be man-made or natural and they show characteristics of both parents. They are always designated by a 'x' in the Latin name.

Opposite leaves Leaves growing in pairs on opposite sides of a stem or twig. This condition is relatively uncommon when compared to the condition known as 'alternate leaves' in which the leaves grow alternately from each side of the twig.

Pollarded A tree is said to be pollarded when it has been cut to the ground several times and has then developed several trunks.

Shelter belt A belt of shrubs or trees planted to form a wind break.

Shoot A new young growth.

Stamens The pollen producing structures of a flower.

Sucker A shoot growing directly from the roots of a tree or shrub; it may be growing some distance from the parent plant and will eventually form a new tree.

Terminal Borne at the end of a stem or twig.

Bay Willow

Deciduous, Small

Primary Features

Leaves glossy, dark green above, white below; only 2–4 times as long as broad, sticky and fragrant when young; growing on very shiny twigs.

Secondary Features

A dense shrub or small tree. Catkins appearing after the leaves, more or less upright, male catkins yellow, female catkins green, later white and fluffy with seed; male and female catkins on separate trees.

Localities and Habits

Streamsides and other wet places.

Lookalikes

Crack Willow p.32; Goat Willow p.136; (Almond Willow p.330).

Flowering and Fruiting Periods

Catkins May–June, seeding in June–July.

White Willow

Deciduous, Medium

Primary Features

Leaves 5–10 times as long as broad, silky white above and below, on ascending branches.

Secondary Features

A medium-sized tree, often pollarded. Catkins appearing with the leaves, male catkins yellow, female catkins green later white and fluffy when in seed, on separate trees.

Localities and Habits

Streamsides and other wet places.

Lookalikes

Crack Willow p.32; (Almond Willow p.330).

Flowering and Fruiting Periods

Catkins April–May, seeding in June.

The White Willow is a medium-sized tree that is often pollarded, and can be found near streams and other water-logged land.

Weeping Willow

Deciduous, Large

Primary Features

Characteristic long, weeping, yellow branches may touch the ground.

Secondary Features

A large tree. Catkins usually male, sometimes with both male and female flowers on the same catkins. Leaves about 10 times as long as broad, green above, whitish below.

Localities and Habits

An introduced hybrid. Commonly planted throughout Europe especially beside water or in gardens.

Lookalikes

(Chinese Weeping Willow p.330).

Flowering and Fruiting Periods

Catkins April–May; no fruit.

The branches of the graceful Weeping Willow tree often hang to the ground forming an elegant backdrop to be planted near ponds or streams.

Violet Willow

Deciduous, Small

Primary Features

Young shoots very distinctive – dark purple, with whitish bloom. Leaves broadly oblong, only 2–4 times as long as broad and with crimson leaf-stalks.

Secondary Features

A shrub or small tree. Catkins appearing before the leaves; almost stalkless, upright, male catkins yellow, female catkins grey-green later white and fluffy when in seed, on separate trees.

Localities and Habits

A northern European native, widely planted in wet places in more southern areas for its purple shoots.

Lookalikes

Goat Willow p.136.

Flowering and Fruiting Periods

Catkins February–March, seeding in May–June.

The dark-purple colour of the young shoots give the Violet Willow its name.

Lookalikes and Cultivars

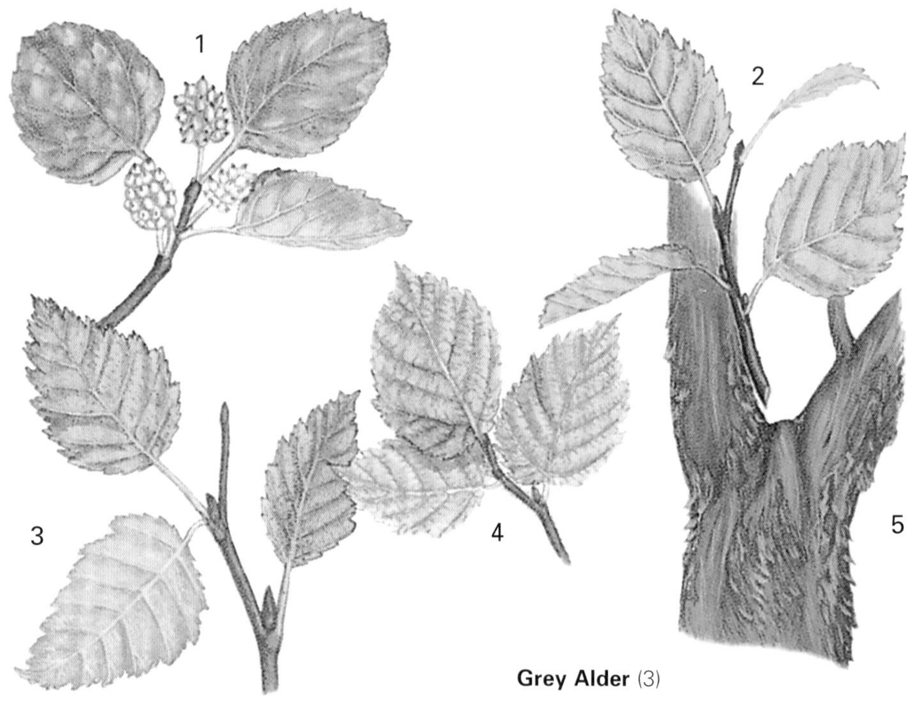

White Mulberry (1)
Leaves shiny, food for silkworms. Fruit white or pink.

Green Alder (2)
Leaves with pronounced double teeth and pointed tips.

Grey Alder (3)
Leaves like those of Green Alder, but grey beneath.

Dutch Elm (4)
A large domed tree with many suckers.

Eastern Strawberry Tree (5)
A Mediterranean tree. Bark reddish-brown, peeling.

Lookalikes and Cultivars

Rhododendron (6)
Flowers large, lilac-purple, in dense clusters.

Citron (7)
Large yellow fruit with thick rind.

Seville Orange (8)
Fruit with sour flesh and thick rough orange rind.

Copper Beech (9)
Leaves distinctive – coppery purple in colour.

Lookalikes and Cultivars

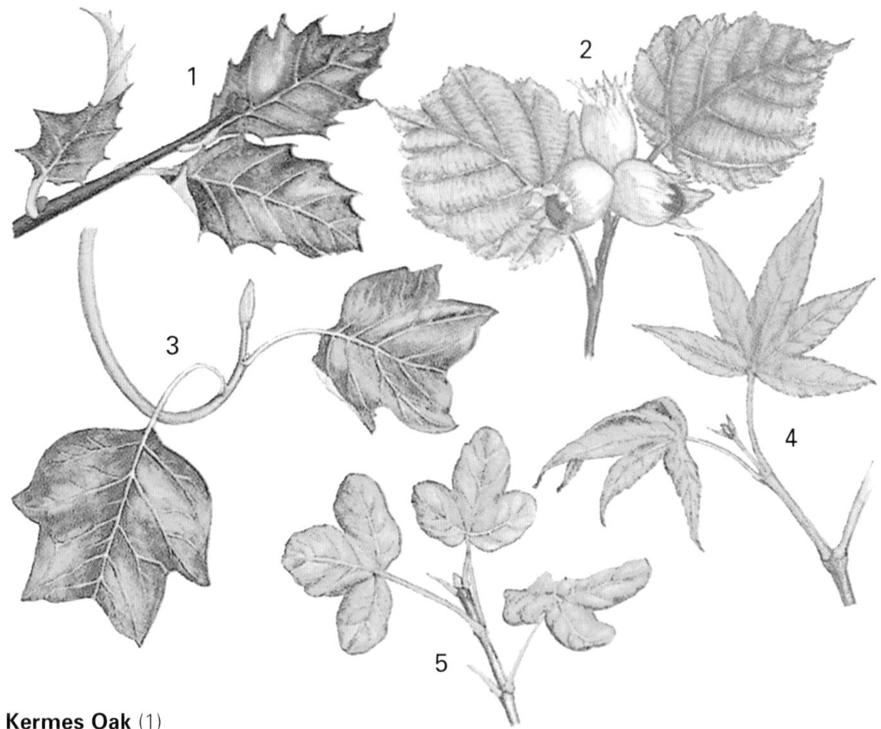

Kermes Oak (1)
A Mediterranean tree. Often a low holly-like bush.

Filbert (2)
Planted for its nuts which are enclosed in green cups.

Tulip Tree (3)
Leaves very distinctive – four-lobed with flat ends.

Japanese Maple (4)
Leaves with up to 11 lobes; a common small garden tree.

Montpelier Maple (5)
A south European tree. Leaves usually with three lobes.

Lookalikes and Cultivars

Midland Hawthorn (6)
Leaves with 3–5 short lobes.
Berries with two or three stones.

Service Tree of Fontainebleau (7)
A western European tree with shallowly lobed leaves.

Narrow-Leaved Ash (8)
A southern European tree; leaves with slender leaflets.

Red Horse Chestnut (9)
A street tree with red flowers; fruits not spiny.

Scotch Laburnum (10)
A small tree with a short trunk.
Seeds are brown.

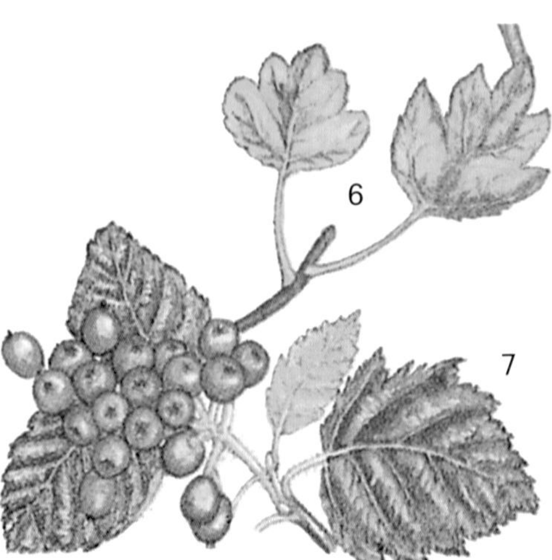

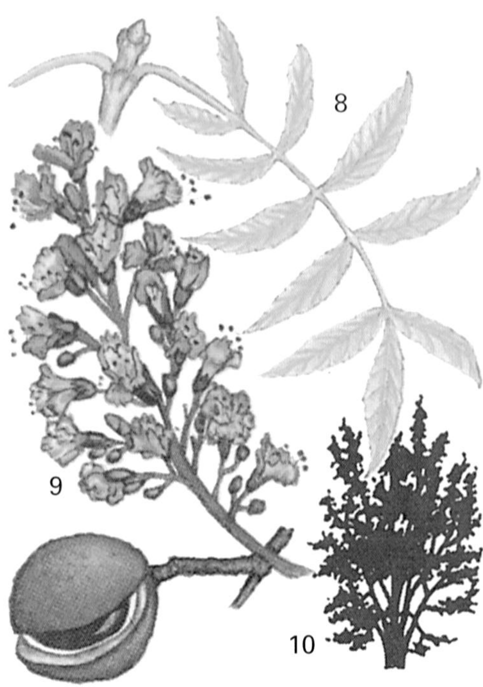

Lookalikes and Cultivars

Spanish Fir (1)
Leaves at right angles to twigs, forming dense cover.

Giant Fir (2)
Needles long, soft and shining, in two rows.

Sitka Spruce (3)
Cones with distinctive curled margins to the scales.

Oriental Spruce (4)
Needles 6–10 mm long, the shortest of any spruce.

Blue Spruce (5)
Needles stout, prickly and very distinctive blue.

Lookalikes and Cultivars

Western Hemlock (6)
Leading tip arched over by up to 60 cm.

Atlas Cedar (7)
Young shoots ascending. Needles in clusters of 10–45.

Monterey Pine (8)
Bright-green soft needles in clusters of 3.

Stone Pine (9)
A Mediterranean tree with sharp dark-green needles.

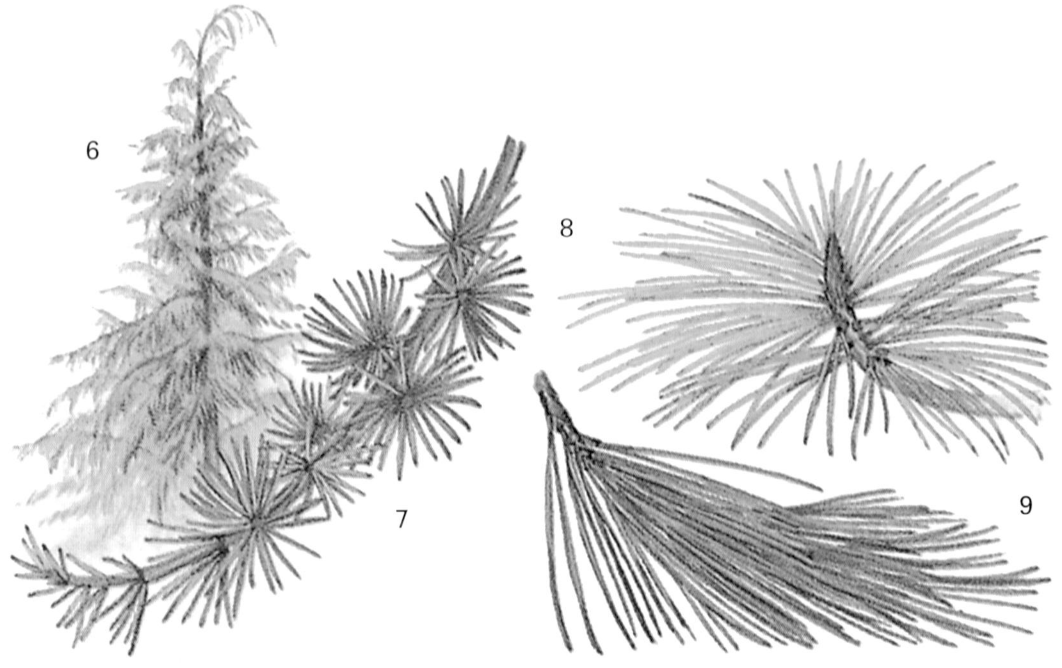

Lookalikes and Cultivars

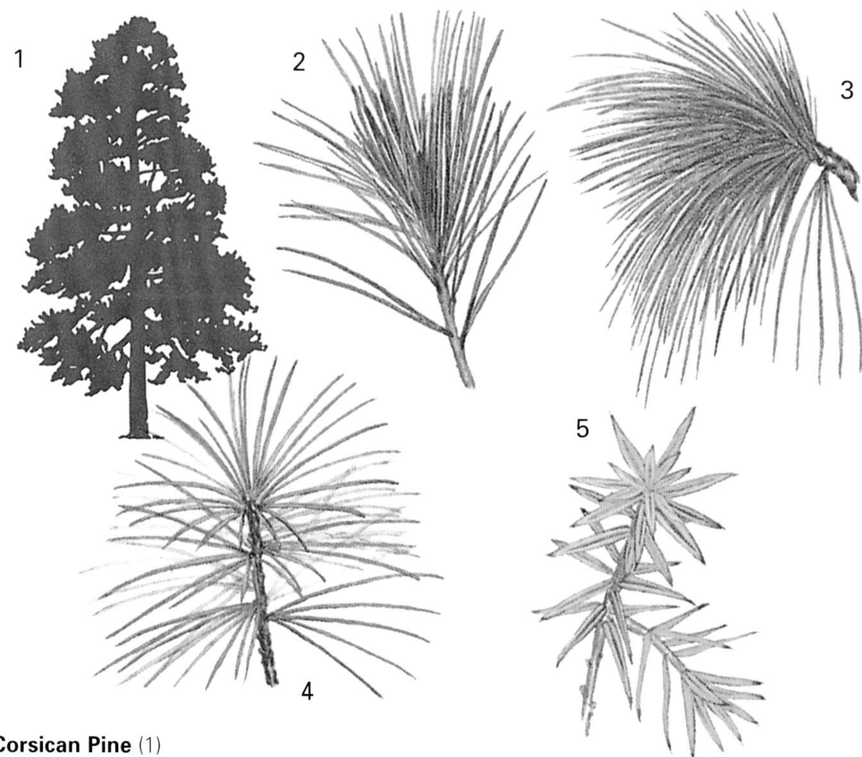

Corsican Pine (1)
A small tree with many level, regular branches.

Aleppo Pine (2)
A Mediterranean tree with pale-grey bark on twigs.

Bhutan Pine (3)
Clusters of five very long, soft, slim needles.

Weymouth Pine (4)
Clusters of five short horizontal blue-green needles.

Prickly Juniper (5)
A shrub with prickly needles having 2 white stripes.

Lookalikes and Cultivars

Pencil Juniper (6)
A tall slender juniper.

Phoenician Juniper (7)
A Mediterranean tree or shrub with scaly branches.

White Cedar (8)
Foliage yellow-green in vertical twisted sprays.

Italian Cypress (9)
A broad columnar tree.

Lookalikes and Cultivars

'Shimidsu Sakura' (2)
Wide spreading branches form a flattened crown.

'Tai-Haku' (3)
Branches spreading. Flowers single, white.

'Hokusai' (4)
One of the earliest to flower. A wide-spreading tree.

JAPANESE CHERRIES (1–7)

'Amanogawa' (1)
Branches ascending to form a very narrow tree.

'Shirotae' (5)
A small tree with drooping branches.

Lookalikes and Cultivars

'Ukon' (6)
A spreading tree with green-tinged flowers.

Cheal's Weeping Cherry (7)
Branches may touch the ground.

MAGNOLIAS

M. grandiflora (8)
An evergreen tree with large leathery leaves.

M. stellata (9)
A small tree. Flowers have many narrow petals.

M. campbelli (10)
A large tree with deep pink flowers.

Lookalikes and Cultivars

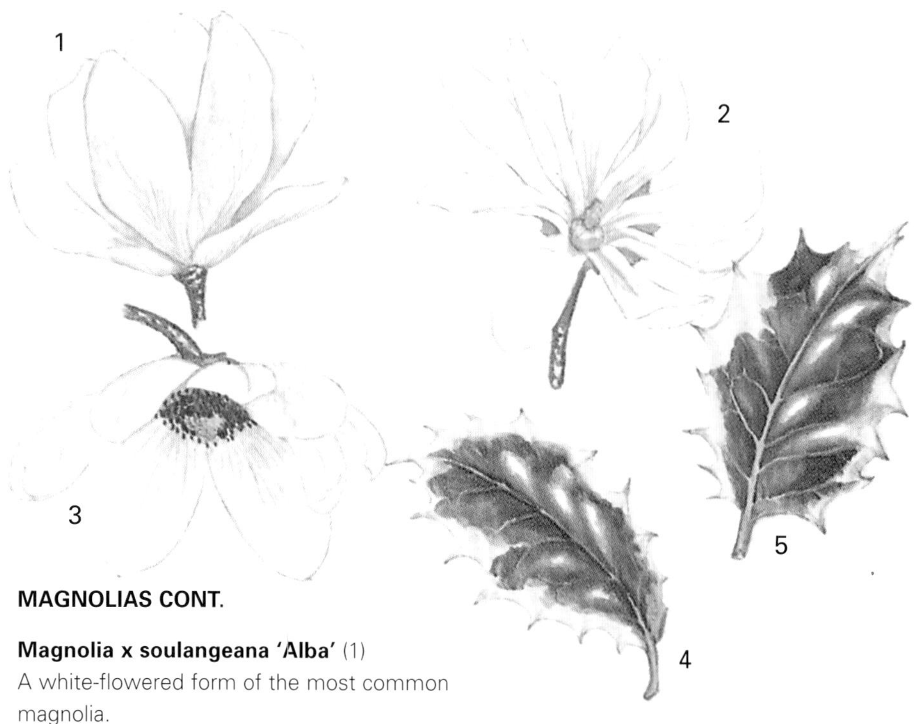

MAGNOLIAS CONT.

Magnolia x soulangeana 'Alba' (1)
A white-flowered form of the most common magnolia.

Magnolia x loebneri 'Merrill' (2)
A small tree with many white flowers.

Magnolia highdownensis (3)
Flowers white, drooping, with central crimson stamens.

HOLLIES

Ilex Argentea Marginata (4)
Leaves have silver edges.

Ilex Aurea Marginata (5)
Leaves have gold edges.

Lookalikes and Cultivars

Hedgehog Holly (6)
Leaves very prickly in centre as well as on edges.

Highclere Holly 'Hodginsii' (7)
Often a part of city hedges.
Leaves with few spines.

EUCALYPTS

Cider Gum (8)
A hardy tree with two very different leaf types.

Australian Snow Gum (9)
Bark like a snake's skin. Leaves large and leathery.

Spinning Gum (10)
A tender tree with two very different leaf types.

Lookalikes and Cultivars

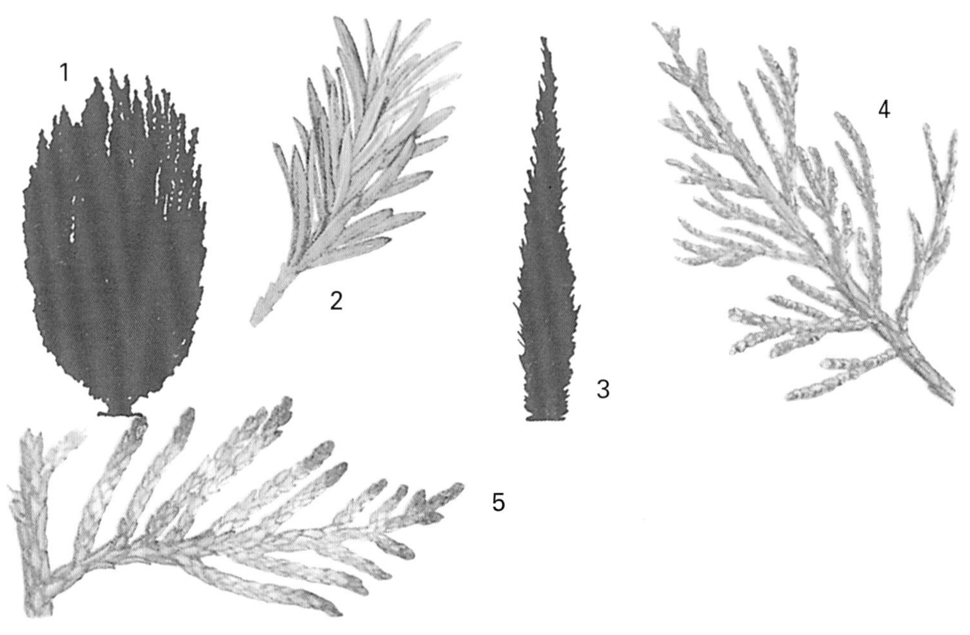

Upright Yew (1)
A narrow upright tree with very dark-green foliage.

Upright Yellow Yew (2)
A narrow upright tree with yellow foliage.

Pencil Juniper 'Skyrocket' (3)
An extremely narrow tree; eventually a tall one.

Monterey Cypress 'Donard Gold' (4)
A conical tree with golden-yellow foliage.

Western Red Cedar 'Zebrina' (5)
A conical tree with green and yellow banded foliage.

Lookalikes and Cultivars

Lawson Cypress 'Pembury Blue' (6)
A conical tree with blue foliage.

Lawson Cypress 'Stewartii' (7)
A conical tree with yellow foliage.

Lawson Cypress 'Pottenii' (8)
A dense conical tree with green foliage.

Lawson Cypress 'Columnaris' (9)
A dense narrow columnar tree with grey-green foliage.

Leyland Cypress 'Castlewellan Gold' (10)
A columnar hedging tree with yellow foliage.

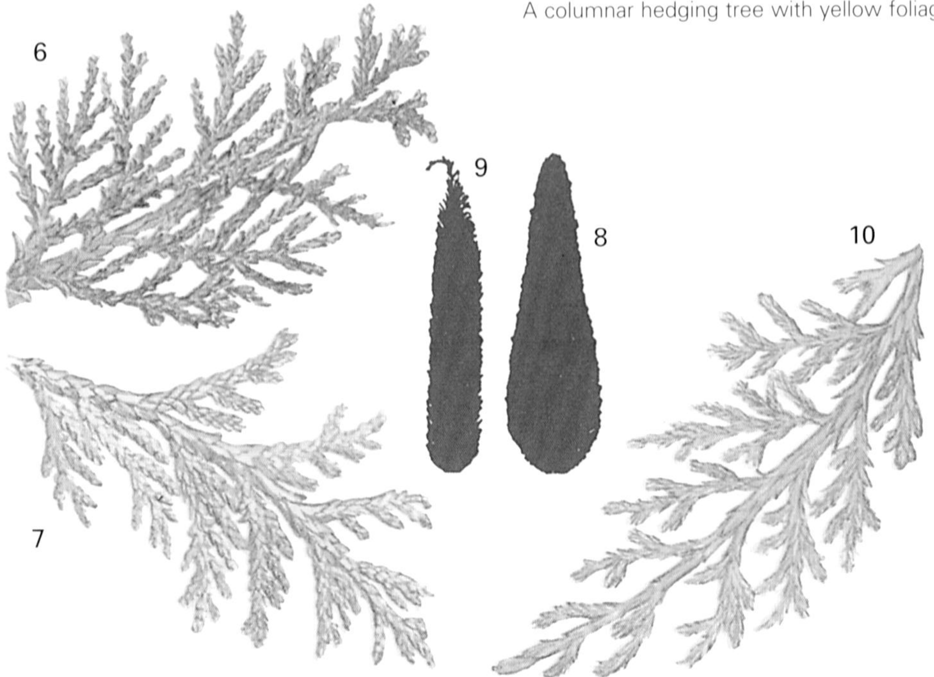

Further Reading

Index and Checklist

Keep a record of your sightings by ticking the boxes.

Crack Willow

Deciduous, Medium

Primary Features

Twigs breaking easily with an audible crack; leaves 4–9 times as long as broad, green above, paler beneath, on spreading, ascending branches.

Secondary Features

A medium-sized tree, often pollarded. Catkins appearing with the leaves; drooping, male catkins yellow, female catkins green later white and fluffy when in seed, on separate trees.

Localities and Habits

Streamsides and other wet places.

Lookalikes

White Willow p.20; (Almond Willow p.330).

Flowering and Fruiting Periods

Catkins April–May, seeding in June–July.

Almond

Deciduous, Small

Primary Features

Flowers light rose-pink, single, solitary or in pairs, appearing before the leaves.

Secondary Features

A small bushy tree bearing leathery, downy, green fruits. Seeds inside the fruit stones are the almonds.

Localities and Habits

Cultivated for its flowers in northern areas and for its nuts in southern areas of Europe.

Lookalikes

(Peach p.330).

Flowering and Fruiting Periods

Flowers February–April; fruit May–July.

The Almond is cultivated for its pretty light rose-pink blossom, and its fruit – almonds – are also prized.

Sloe or Blackthorn

Deciduous, Small

Primary Features

Flowers white, solitary, appearing before the leaves on short spine-tipped side branches – very striking against the blackish bark.

Secondary Features

A dense, suckering shrub or small tree. Leaves dull green above, somewhat downy below, especially on the veins. Fruit is the sloe – small bluish-black acid berries with a definite bloom.

Localities and Habits

Forms dense thickets in hedgerows and woodland all over Europe except the extreme north.

Lookalikes

Cherry Plum p.64.

Flowering and Fruiting Periods

Flowers March–April; fruit September–October.

The attractive bluish-black berries of the Sloe or Blackthorn tree can be found in hedgerows all over Europe in the autumn.

Plum

Deciduous, Small

Primary Features

Fruit is the plum – sweet, juicy fruits, 2–7.5 cm long, yellow, red or purple in colour, drooping, in small clusters or solitary.

Secondary Features

A small tree or suckering shrub. Flowers occur in clusters of two or three, appearing with the leaves. Petals white, often have a greenish tinge, especially in bud. Leaves dull green above, almost smooth beneath.

Localities and Habits

Grown for its fruit and often naturalized in hedgerows all over Europe.

Lookalikes

Cherry Plum p.64; (Copper Beech p.335).

Flowering and Fruiting Periods

Flowers March–May; fruit July–October.

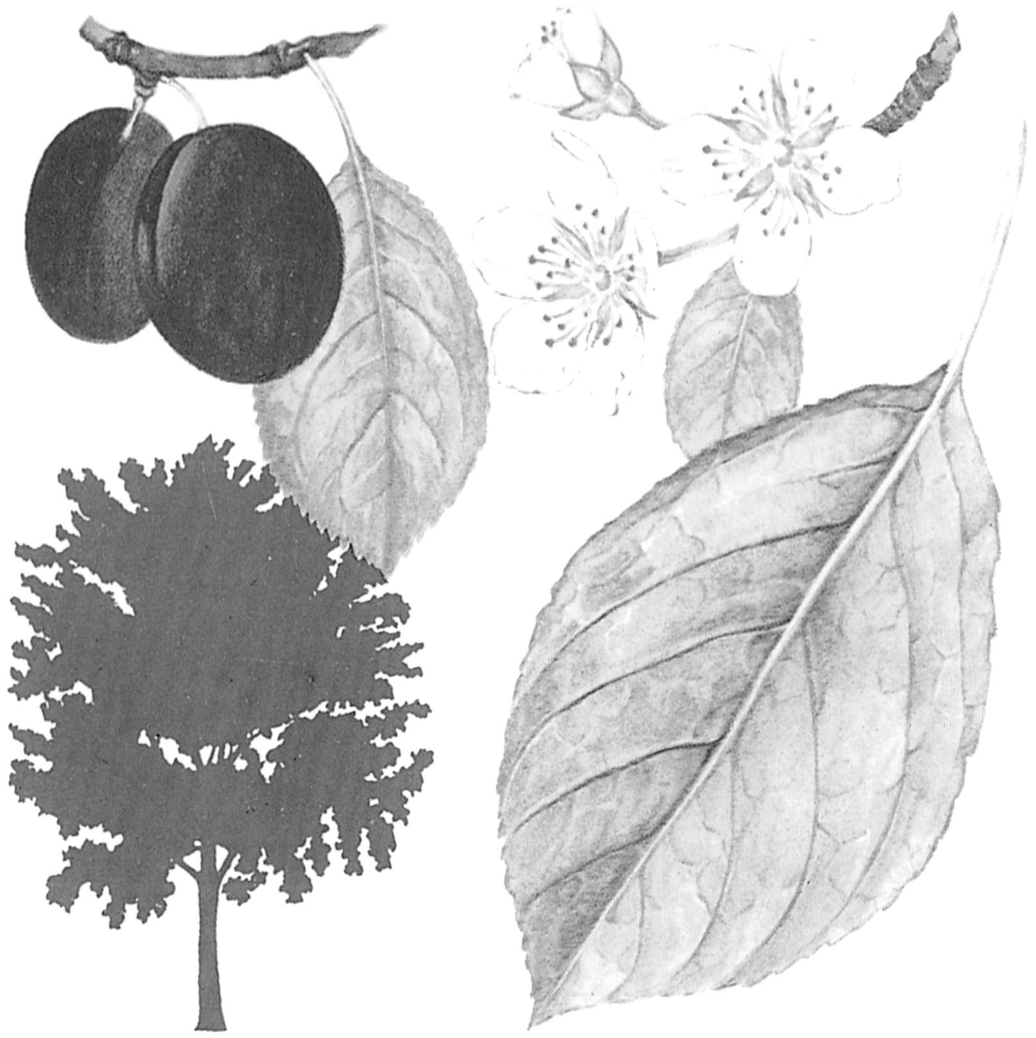

Plum trees can be found in hedgerows as well as orchards and its juicy fruit ripens in the late summer and autumn months.

Pear

Deciduous, Medium

Primary Features

Fruit is the pear – small, brownish in the wild tree, but garden escapes are common and these may have bigger, more yellow fruit.

Secondary Features

A medium-sized tree with ascending branches. Clusters of about five white flowers appear before the leaves are fully open; naturalized trees may have mistletoe growing on them.

Localities and Habits

Hedgerows or orchards. Cultivated forms are grown in gardens and orchards.

Lookalikes

Crab Apple p.62.

Flowering and Fruiting Periods

Flowers April–May; fruit July–October.

Bird Cherry

Deciduous, Medium

Primary Features

Flowers white, bell-shaped, fragrant, in long drooping chains.

Secondary Features

A medium-sized tree with greyish-brown, peeling bark which has a strong foetid smell. Fruits are blue-black, bitter cherries, each about 8 mm in length, in drooping chains.

Localities and Habits

Found in most European countries especially on lime-rich soils. Planted in streets and gardens.

Lookalikes

(Rum Cherry p.330).

Flowering and Fruiting Periods

Flowers May; fruit July–September.

The Bird Cherry's peeling bark releases a strong foetid smell, while the delicate chains of blossom are fragrant.

Portuguese Laurel

Evergreen, Small

Primary Features

Distinctive red leaf-stalks on long, leathery, dark-green leaves.

Secondary Features

A dense, domed shrub or small tree. Flowers small, fragrant, creamy white in many-flowered spikes; fruit very small, brownish berries, in long chains.

Localities and Habits

Native to parts of southern Europe and widely planted, especially as a hedge, further north.

Lookalikes

Cherry Laurel p.158; Sweet Bay p.162.

Flowering and Fruiting Periods

Flowers June; fruit August–October.

The Portuguese Laurel is native to southern Europe, but popular for hedges further north, too.

Spindle Tree

Deciduous, Small

Primary Features

Fruits are deep pink, four-lobed capsules, opening to expose seeds in bright-orange seed covers.

Secondary Features

A shrub or small tree with many branches. Leaves opposite, lance-shaped. Flowers greenish-yellow in small clusters in axils of leaves.

Localities and Habits

Woods, hedgerows and scrub, especially on lime-rich soils, over much of Europe except the north and south.

Lookalikes

Japanese Spindle Tree p.330.

Flowering and Fruiting Periods

Flowers May–June; fruit September–October.

The fruits of the Spindle Tree are a rich pink colour and the seeds have bright-orange covers.

Buckthorn

Deciduous, Small

Primary Features

Fruits are round, purple-black berries with yellow pips, occurring singly or in small clusters.

Secondary Features

A shrub or small tree. Twigs bear opposite leaves and end in thorns. Flowers are sweetly scented, small, greenish, in small clusters at the bases of the young shoots; male and female flowers on separate trees.

Localities and Habits

Hedges and scrub over much of Europe except the Mediterranean region.

Lookalikes

Alder Buckthorn p.140.

Flowering and Fruiting Periods

Flowers May–June; fruit August–September.

Crab Apple

Deciduous, Small

Primary Features

Fruit is small, reddish-yellow apple, sour and hard.

Secondary Features

A small tree. Flowers form in clusters of 3–4, white, suffused with pink, appearing with the leaves on short side branches. Occasionally may have mistletoe growing on it.

Localities and Habits

Hedgerows, scrub, woodland, over much of Europe. Naturalized cultivated apples have larger, sweeter fruit.

Lookalikes

Pear p.46.

Flowering and Fruiting Periods

Flowers May; fruit September–October.

Cherry Plum

Deciduous, Small

Primary Features

Fruit smooth, round, sweet, red or yellow, 2–3.5 cm long, growing singly, but not always produced in more northern areas.

Secondary Features

A shrub or small round-headed tree. White flowers are solitary or in clusters of 2–3, appearing with the leaves; usually the first cherry to flower. A purple-leaved form with pink flowers is commonly planted.

Localities and Habits

Often grown in streets and gardens, also cultivated for its fruit.

Lookalikes

Blackthorn p.38; Plum p.42.

Flowering and Fruiting Periods

Flowers March; fruit July–September.

Wayfaring Tree

Deciduous, Small

Primary Features

Flowers creamy white, tubular, in large, flat clusters on the ends of shoots.

Secondary Features

A shrub or small tree. Leaves rounded, opposite, wrinkled, felted on both surfaces but felting persisting only on lower surface. Fruit a flat cluster of many oval berries, red at first later black.

Localities and Habits

Hedges, thickets, edges of woods throughout much of Europe except extreme north.

Lookalikes

None.

Flowering and Fruiting Periods

Flowers May–June; fruit September onwards.

The creamy-white flat clusters of flowers belonging to the Wayfaring Tree give way to clusters of oval-shaped fruit, that turn from red to black.

Snowy Mespilus

Deciduous, Small

Primary Features

Very distinctive appearance in spring, when opening buds have a whitish appearance because of the white under-surfaces of the young leaves and the white flower buds.

Secondary Features

A shrub or small tree. White star-like flowers occur in small upright clusters in the axils of the leaves. Fruits are small berries, red at first, later blue-black, often occurring singly.

Localities and Habits

Open woodland, limestone uplands, over much of Europe. Often planted in parks and gardens.

Lookalikes

Several other very similar species of mespilus are grown in Europe.

Flowering and Fruiting Periods

Flowers April–May; fruit July–August.

Gean or Wild Cherry

Deciduous, Medium

Primary Features

Clusters of 2–6 small cherries, at first yellow flushed with red then dark purple-red unless eaten by birds first.

Secondary Features

A medium-sized tree with many suckers, and reddish-brown bark. Flowers white in dense clusters, appearing just before the leaves.

Localities and Habits

Found over much of Europe except extreme north and south; a double-flowered variety is often planted in gardens.

Lookalikes

Japanese Cherries p.76, p.342–43; (Sour Cherry p.331).

Flowering and Fruiting Periods

Flowers April–May; fruit June.

The white blossom of the Gean or Wild Cherry often comes in a double-flowered variety.

Japanese Cherries

Deciduous, Medium

Primary Features

Flowers large, bright pink (white or light pink in some varieties), double or semi-double, in clusters, usually opening just before the leaves.

Secondary Features

A large group of medium-sized trees often with spreading or even horizontal branches. Many have bronze-coloured young leaves. They are usually sterile.

Localities and Habits

Introduced and cultivated varieties widely planted in streets and gardens throughout Europe.

Lookalikes

Many different varieties, see page 342–43; Gean p.72.

Flowering and Fruiting Periods

Flowers April–May; no fruit.

Variety illustrated is 'Kanzan'

Lombardy Poplar

Deciduous, Medium

Primary Features

Branches all ascending to give a very characteristic narrow outline to this medium-sized tree.

Secondary Features

Trees almost all male; male catkins reddish, not fluffy. Leaves often triangular in outline, leaf-stalks yellow-green in colour, flattened.

Localities and Habits

Frequently planted as windbreaks over much of Europe especially in lowland areas.

Lookalikes

(Black Poplar p.331; Black Italian Poplar p.331).

Flowering and Fruiting Periods

Flowers March–April; no fruit.

Downy Birch

Deciduous, Small/Medium

Primary Features

Female flowering catkins grey-green; male catkins bright yellow; seeds numerous, winged, not fluffy, in greenish-brown fruiting catkins.

Secondary Features

A small- or medium-sized tree with one or several trunks. Bark greyish-white with brown horizontal bands. Male and female catkins on same tree. Young twigs and leaf-stalks covered with soft down, leaves often diamond-shaped.

Localities and Habits

Northern Europe and southern European mountain areas on poor acid soils.

Lookalikes

Silver Birch p.116.

Flowering and Fruiting Periods

Catkins April–May, seeding in July–August.

Small-Leaved Lime

Deciduous, Large

Primary Features

Characteristic flying bracts at first bear small clusters of yellowish-white flowers, later clusters of small ribless, thin-shelled nutlets, both on the upper side.

Secondary Features

A large tree, often with bosses on its otherwise smooth trunk – areas of twigs and short shoots. Leaves 3–6 cm long, heart-shaped with pointed tips.

Localities and Habits

Grows wild throughout much of Europe except extreme north; also planted as a street tree.

Lookalikes

Large-Leaved Lime p.84; Common Lime p.88.

Flowering and Fruiting Periods

Flowers July; fruit August–September.

Large-Leaved Lime

Deciduous, Large

Primary Features

Characteristic flying bracts at first bear small clusters of yellowish-white flowers, later clusters of small heavily ribbed, woody nutlets, both from the lower side.

Secondary Features

A large tree with a smooth, grey trunk, bosses very rare. Leaves 6–12 cm long, heart-shaped with pointed tips.

Localities and Habits

Native to central and southern Europe; extensively planted as a street tree in more northern areas.

Lookalikes

Small-Leaved Lime p.82; Common Lime p.88.

Flowering and Fruiting Periods

Flowers June; fruit July–September.

The heart-shaped leaves of the Large-Leaved Lime have helped it become a favourite tree in towns and cities.

Common Lime

Deciduous, Large

Primary Features

Characteristic flying bracts at first bear small clusters of yellowish-white flowers, later clusters of small slightly ribbed, woody nutlets, both from its lower side.

Secondary Features

A large tree in which the trunk is covered with bosses – large areas of twigs and shoots. Leaves 6–10 cm long, heart-shaped with pointed tips, often infested with aphids, which drip honeydew on to the ground beneath.

Localities and Habits

Often occurs in the wild as a hybrid of the other two limes. Frequently planted as a street tree.

Lookalikes

Small-Leaved Lime p.82; Large-Leaved Lime p.84.

Flowering and Fruiting Periods

Flowers July; fruit August–September.

Black Mulberry

Deciduous, Small

Primary Features

Fruit a dense cylindrical cluster of many berries, 2–2.5 cm long, at first green, ripening to deep red, berries very acid until ripe.

Secondary Features

A low, domed tree with large rough, sometimes almost lobed leaves. Young shoots with milky juice. Male and female flowers pale green, in separate spikes, both very small and on same tree.

Localities and Habits

Cultivated for its fruit in much of Europe; occasionally naturalized.

Lookalikes

(White Mulberry p.334).

Flowering and Fruiting Periods

Flowers May; fruit July–September.

The Black Mulberry is a low, gnarled tree with large edible, cylindrical berries and is grown in many parts of Europe.

Strawberry Tree

Evergreen, Small

Primary Features

Flowers white, bell-shaped in hanging clusters appearing in autumn, together with the ripening berries from the previous year.

Secondary Features

A wide-topped small- to medium-sized tree with brown fibrous bark and leathery, dark-green leaves. Berries are rounded and warty, yellow at first ripening to deep red.

Localities and Habits

Thickets and the edges of woodland, especially on hillsides in southern and western Europe.

Lookalikes

(Eastern Strawberry Tree p.334).

Flowering and Fruiting Periods

Flowers and fruit October–December.

Aspen

Deciduous, Medium

Primary Features

Male catkins fluffy and brown with yellow pollen; female catkins purple at first, later white and fluffy with seed; the two kinds of catkin are on separate trees.

Secondary Features

A medium-sized tree with many suckers. Often called Trembling Aspen from the constant shivering of the leaves – this caused by the very flattened, whitish leaf-stalks.

Localities and Habits

Forms thickets on poor, damp soils especially in northern and mountain areas.

Lookalikes

Grey Poplar p.110; (Black Poplar p.331).

Flowering and Fruiting Periods

Catkins February–March; seeding in May.

The Aspen is often called the Trembling Aspen due to its quivering leaves.

Southern Nettle-Tree

Deciduous, Medium

Primary Features

Characteristic nettle-shaped leaves have long, twisted tips. Small, yellow, solitary flowers grow on long stalks in the axils of the leaves in late spring.

Secondary Features

A medium-sized, round-headed tree. Fruits are small, solitary, brown berries, growing on long stalks in the axils of the leaves.

Localities and Habits

Native to southern Europe where it is often planted as a street tree.

Lookalikes

None.

Flowering and Fruiting Periods

Flowers May; fruit September.

Whitebeam

Deciduous, Medium

Primary Features

Young shoots, leaves and flower-stalks all covered in dense white wool; leaves retaining a white woolly underside all summer.

Secondary Features

A medium-sized tree or large shrub. Flowers white in large, flat clusters; fruit bright-red berries in similar clusters. Leaves very variable in shape, some almost lobed or with very deep teeth.

Localities and Habits

Grows throughout much of Europe especially on chalk; often planted as a street tree.

Lookalikes

Swedish Whitebeam p.226; Wild Service Tree p.228.

Flowering and Fruiting Periods

Flowers May–June; fruit September–October.

As its name suggests, the Whitebeam is noted for the woolly white covering on its young shoots, leaves and flower-stalks.

Sweet Chestnut

Deciduous, Large

Primary Features

Spiny green cups split open to reveal several deep-brown shining nuts.

Secondary Features

A large tree with wide spreading branches. Leaves large, up to 25 cm long. Flowers in bisexual catkins, a few green female flowers at the base, yellow male flowers along most of the length of the catkins.

Localities and Habits

Cultivated and naturalized over most of Europe.

Lookalikes

None.

Flowering and Fruiting Periods

Flowers July; fruit October.

The edible fruit of the Sweet Chestnut tree can be roasted for an autumn or winter treat and can be grown over most of Europe.

Grey Poplar

Deciduous, Large

Primary Features

Male catkins reddish with grey fur and yellow pollen; female catkins rare; the two kinds of catkin on separate trees.

Secondary Features

A large spreading tree with many suckers. Young leaves grey-downy, the down not persisting. Summer leaves on the suckers simple, not lobed, but with deep teeth. Female catkins when present, green, later white and fluffy with seed.

Localities and Habits

Wet woodland in much of Europe; mostly spreading by means of suckers.

Lookalikes

White Poplar p.208; Aspen p.96.

Flowering and Fruiting Periods

Catkins February–March, seeding in April.

The Grey Poplar spreads by means of suckers. Interestingly, the male and rare female catkins grow on separate trees.

Alder

Deciduous, Medium

Primary Features

Fruiting catkins are dark brown and stalked, like small cones, and remain on the tree after the winged seeds have gone until the following year.

Secondary Features

A medium-sized tree. Leaves almost round. Male catkins in small clusters, purple in winter, yellow in spring; female catkins purple, becoming green in fruit, then brown and woody.

Localities and Habits

Beside water and in fens throughout most of Europe.

Lookalikes

(Green Alder p.334; Grey Alder p.334).

Flowering and Fruiting Periods

Catkins February–April, fruiting catkins persistent.

Silver Birch

Deciduous, Medium

Primary Features

Both smooth, silvery white and peeling with black diamond-shaped markings. Smaller branches drooping.

Secondary Features

A medium-sized tree. Male catkins in clusters, brownish in winter, yellow with pollen in spring; female catkins grey-green in winter, brownish-green in spring, both on the same tree. Seeds with two wings, numerous.

Localities and Habits

Grows on acid soils over much of Europe.

Lookalikes

Downy Birch p.80.

Flowering and Fruiting Periods

Catkins April–May, seeding in July–August.

The Silver Birch is characterised by its silver-white bark, which peels off to reveal black horizontal markings.

Hazel or Cobnut

Deciduous, Small

Primary Features

Male catkins long and yellow in drooping clusters; female flowers tiny red spikes appearing just after the male catkins of the same plant have shed their pollen.

Secondary Features

A shrub or small tree with ascending branches. Leaves almost round. Fruits grow in green cups with ragged edges.

Localities and Habits

Hedgerows, woodlands and in gardens throughout Europe.

Lookalikes

(Filbert p.336).

Flowering and Fruiting Periods

Flowers January–April; fruit September–October.

The fruit of the Hazel or Cobnut tree is enjoyed by people and wildlife alike in the autumn.

Wych Elm

Deciduous, Large

Primary Features

Leaves 8–16 cm long, very rough, with one side having an ear-like projection at the base which covers the very short leaf-stalk.

Secondary Features

A large domed tree with no suckers. Flowers dark-purple clusters; fruits round and winged with a central seed, numerous.

Localities and Habits

Woods and hedgerows throughout much of Europe before Dutch Elm Disease destroyed the trees of whole areas.

Lookalikes

English Elm p.126; Smooth Elm p.128; (Dutch Elm p.334).

Flowering and Fruiting Periods

Flowers February–March; fruit May–July.

English Elm

Deciduous, Large

Primary Features

Leaves 4.5–9 cm long and rough; ear-like projection at the base of one side of the leaf which does not cover the leaf-stalk.

Secondary Features

A large tree with a narrow crown and many suckers and twigs growing from the trunk. Many clusters of dark-red flowers are borne, however fruits are not always formed or are often sterile.

Localities and Habits

Very characteristic of hedgerows before Dutch Elm Disease wiped out whole areas of trees.

Lookalikes

Wych Elm p.124; Smooth Elm p.128; (Dutch Elm p.334).

Flowering and Fruiting Periods

Flowers February–March; fruit May–June (if produced).

Smooth Elm

Deciduous, Large

Primary Features

Leaves 2.5–11.5 cm long and smooth. Ear-like projection at base of one side of the leaf does not cover the leaf-stalk or may not be present at all.

Secondary Features

A large tree with a narrow crown and many suckers and twigs growing from the trunk. Flowers are red clusters but fruit is rarely produced.

Localities and Habits

Native to much of Europe and often planted as a street tree before Dutch Elm Disease.

Lookalikes

Wych Elm p.124; English Elm p.126; (Dutch Elm p.334).

Flowering and Fruiting Periods

Flowers February–March; fruit April–May (if produced).

Hornbeam

Deciduous, Medium

Primary Features

Fruiting spike consists of about eight pairs of small nuts, each one cupped in a three-lobed bract, at first green later brown, the whole making a loose bunch.

Secondary Features

A medium-sized tree in which the twigs grow horizontally in a zig-zag pattern. Male catkins up to 5 cm long, greenish-yellow, drooping. Female catkins about 2 cm long, green, drooping.

Localities and Habits

Hedgerows, woods, sometimes coppiced; sometimes planted as a street tree. Over much of Europe.

Lookalikes

Hop Hornbeam p.134; Beech p.142.

Flowering and Fruiting Periods

Flowers April–May; fruit July–October.

The twigs of the Hornbeam grow horizontally in a zig-zag pattern. The male catkins are more than twice the size of the female catkins.

Hop Hornbeam

Deciduous, Medium

Primary Features

Fruiting spike consists of about 15 small nuts, each one enclosed in a bladder, at first green later whitish, the whole forming a tight bunch.

Secondary Features

A medium-sized tree, sometimes with several trunks. The male catkins are up to 10 cm long, yellow and drooping. The female catkins are small, green, amongst the emerging leaves.

Localities and Habits

Woodlands and well-drained slopes in southern Europe; occasionally introduced further north.

Lookalikes

Hornbeam p.130.

Flowering and Fruiting Periods

Flowers April; fruit September–October.

Goat Willow

Deciduous, Small

Primary Features

Male catkins conspicuous on bare branches, upright, stalkless, silvery at first, yellow with pollen later.

Secondary Features

A shrub or small tree. Female catkins upright, stalkless, green at first, appearing before the leaves, later white and fluffy with seed. Male and female catkins on separate trees.

Localities and Habits

Woodlands, hedgerows and scrub over much of Britain and continental Europe.

Lookalikes

(Grey Willow p.331); Violet Willow p.28.

Flowering and Fruiting Periods

Catkins March–April, seeding in May.

The male catkin of the Goat Willow is yellow with pollen, whereas female catkins grow on separate trees and later turn white and fluffy.

Alder Buckthorn

Deciduous, Small

Primary Features

Round berries, solitary or in pairs, grow on stalks from the axils of leaves, yellow at first, later red, then black.

Secondary Features

A shrub or small tree. Twigs thornless with alternate leaves. Flowers small, white-green, solitary or in pairs in the axils of the leaves.

Localities and Habits

Moist heathland and fens, damp open woodland throughout much of Europe except the extreme north and south.

Lookalikes

Buckthorn p.60.

Flowering and Fruiting Periods

Flowers May–June; fruit July–November.

Beech

Deciduous, Large

Primary Features

Spiky brown cupules split into four lobes to reveal shiny brown three-angled nuts – the beech nuts.

Secondary Features

A large tree. Leaves oval with pointed tips and wavy margins, very bright distinctive green when young. Male flowers pale-yellow clusters, female flowers in pairs, green, both appearing with the leaves on the same tree.

Localities and Habits

Beechwoods are common on well-drained soils throughout Europe particularly on chalk.

Lookalikes

Hornbeam p.130; (Copper Beech p.335).

Flowering and Fruiting Periods

Flowers May; fruit September–October.

The nuts of the Beech tree are edible, but are more popular with wildlife than humans.

Holm Oak

Evergreen, Large

Primary Features

Fruit an acorn. Leaves entire with wavy margins and occasional spines; dark green above and grey-furry below.

Secondary Features

A large tree with a dense evergreen crown. Male catkins long and drooping, pale green, later gold with pollen; female flowers small, greenish-grey and furry.

Localities and Habits

Native to the Mediterranean region and widely grown in more northern areas of Europe.

Lookalikes

Cork Oak p.150; (Kermes Oak p.336).

Flowering and Fruiting Periods

Flowers June, acorns ripen in October.

The leaves of the Holm Oak are wavy, rather than the lobe-edged ones of the Common Oak.

Cork Oak

Evergreen, Medium

Primary Features

Fruit an acorn. Leaves entire with wavy, spiny margins, dark green above, grey and furry below.

Secondary Features

A medium-sized tree with a heavy, dense crown. Bark is thick with commercial cork, which is stripped off leaving bare red wood. Male catkins green, in clusters; female flowers small, in axils of new leaves.

Localities and Habits

Dry hills of the Mediterranean region; widely planted for its cork.

Lookalikes

Holm Oak p.146; (Kermes Oak p.336).

Flowering and Fruiting Periods

Flowers April–May, acorns ripen in October.

Medlar

Deciduous, Small

Primary Features

Fruit brown and oval like a rose-hip, at first hard, later becoming soft and edible – the medlar.

Secondary Features

Wild form a crooked, thorny shrub; cultivated form a thornless tree. Young twigs, leaves and flower-stalks covered with fine white down. Flowers large, solitary, with five white petals.

Localities and Habits

Wild form grows in hedgerows and woodlands in much of Europe except the north, cultivated form in gardens.

Lookalikes

None.

Flowering and Fruiting Periods

Flowers May–June; fruit September–November.

Quince

Deciduous, Small

Primary Features

Fruit hard; pear-shaped or round; yellow, sweet smelling when ripe – the quince.

Secondary Features

A small tree. Young twigs and undersides of leaves white and woolly. Flowers solitary, pink, bowl-shaped, borne in the axils of the leaves.

Localities and Habits

Hedgerows and copses and grown in gardens for its fruit in much of Britain and continental Europe, especially the southern areas.

Lookalikes

(Japonica p.331).

Flowering and Fruiting Periods

Flowers May; fruit September–October.

The fragrant fruit of the Quince can be used in desserts and preserves, but it remains much harder than the apples or pears that it resembles.

Cherry Laurel

Evergreen, Small

Primary Features

Large, leathery, evergreen leaves have pale-green leaf-stalks; flowers in an upright spike, creamy white.

Secondary Features

A spreading shrub or small tree, often wider than tall. Fruit small, black, juicy berries in a chain. All parts of the plant are poisonous.

Localities and Habits

Widely planted in parks and gardens in much of Britain and continental Europe and often naturalized.

Lookalikes

Portuguese Laurel p.52; Sweet Bay p.162; (Rhododendron p.335).

Flowering and Fruiting Periods

Flowers April; fruit August–September.

The upright spikes of Cherry Laurel's flowers develop into juicy black berries and, although the tree is widely planted, all parts of it are poisonous.

Sweet Bay or Bay Laurel

Evergreen, Medium

Primary Features

Dark-green, leathery, evergreen leaves have dark-red leaf-stalks and an aromatic scent when crushed – widely used in cooking.

Secondary Features

A dense shrub or small tree. Flowers small, pale yellow, in pairs in the axils of the leaves. Fruits are green berries, later turning black.

Localities and Habits

A native of the Mediterranean and often planted for ornament there and further north; not hardy.

Lookalikes

Portuguese Laurel p.52; Cherry Laurel p.158.

Flowering and Fruiting Periods

Flowers March–April; fruit August–October.

Lilac

Deciduous, Small

Primary Features

Characteristic flowers in large cones, pink, white or purple, fragrant; each flower is tubular in shape.

Secondary Features

A shrub or small tree with many suckers. Leaves opposite, hairless, yellow-green, large and rounded. Fruit a cluster of brown capsules.

Localities and Habits

Scrub in Balkans; widely cultivated in gardens and parks; sometimes naturalized in hedgerows.

Lookalikes

None.

Flowering and Fruiting Periods

Flowers May–June; fruit September.

Magnolia

Deciduous, Small

Primary Features

Flowers large, cup-shaped, solitary, with a multitude of white or pink petals, borne at the tips of the shoots.

Secondary Features

Mostly low-growing, spreading trees but some medium-sized species and some species evergreen. Leaves large and dark green above, often furry below.

Localities and Habits

A large group of introduced trees widely planted for ornament.

Lookalikes

(About 35 species of magnolias, see page 343. Tulip Tree p.336).

Flowering and Fruiting Periods

Flowers in spring, summer or autumn depending on species.

Variety illustrated is Magnolia x soulangeana

All varieties of Magnolia are noted for their luxurious waxy petals, which appear in spring, summer or autumn, depending on the species.

Box

Evergreen, Small

Primary Features

Branches clothed in very small, opposite, dark-green, glossy leaves with pale-orange, hairy leaf-stalks.

Secondary Features

A shrub or small tree. Flowers small, greenish-yellow in clusters in axils of leaves. Fruits small, greyish, rounded capsules.

Localities and Habits

Cultivated varieties used in hedges in much of Europe except extreme north; a native of southern hillsides.

Lookalikes

None.

Flowering and Fruiting Periods

Flowers March–April; fruit August–September.

The Box is often used for the 'skeleton' of formal gardens, providing orderlines even in winter due to its evergreen leaves.

Holly

Evergreen, Small

Primary Features

Fruits are red berries in clusters in the axils of the leaves in mid-winter.

Secondary Features

A shrub or small tree. Leaves with prickly edges, dark green and glossy above, paler beneath. Flowers white, fragrant, in clusters in axils of the leaves.

Localities and Habits

In beech or oak woodland in much of Europe and often cultivated in shelter belts or as a hedge.

Lookalikes

(There are many cultivated varieties of holly with different colours and spines on the leaves, see p.344–45.)

Flowering and Fruiting Periods

Flowers May–June; fruit November–December.

Holly grows in much of Europe, both in the wild and in cultivated forms.

Lemon

Evergreen, Small

Primary Features

Fruit oval, pale yellow, with a distinctive scent and sour flesh – the lemon.

Secondary Features

A small tree. Leaves thin and leathery, sometimes with irregular teeth; leaf-stalks are narrowly winged. Twigs bear pointed, green thorns. Flowers white, flushed with red, solitary and sweetly scented.

Localities and Habits

Cultivated throughout the Mediterranean region.

Lookalikes

(Citron p.335).

Flowering and Fruiting Periods

Flowers in spring; fruit end autumn (native climes).

Sweet Orange

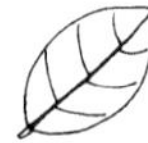

Evergreen, Small

Primary Features

Fruit rounded, orange-yellow, with a distinctive scent and sweet flesh.

Secondary Features

A small tree. Leaves thin and leathery, with wavy margins and narrowly winged leaf-stalks. Twigs not thorny. Flowers white, solitary and sweetly scented.

Localities and Habits

Cultivated for its fruit throughout the Mediterranean region.

Lookalikes

(Seville Orange p.335).

Flowering and Fruiting Periods

Flowers in spring; fruit end autumn and winter (native climes).

Judas Tree

Deciduous, Small

Primary Features

Flowers bright pink, pea-like, in clusters, appearing before the leaves, growing directly out of larger branches as well as from smaller twigs.

Secondary Features

A small tree. Leaves almost round or kidney-shaped. Fruits like pea-pods, dark red or brown, in clusters.

Localities and Habits

Dry rocky areas in the Mediterranean region. Introduced into gardens and parks in more northern areas.

Lookalikes

None.

Flowering and Fruiting Periods

Flowers March–May; fruit July–September.

Olive

Evergreen, Small

Primary Features

Fruits are edible, succulent and oily, green at first, turning black over the course of the following year.

Secondary Features

A small gnarled tree. Leaves opposite. Flowers white, fragrant, in chains in the axils of the leaves.

Localities and Habits

Open woodland and thickets on rocky hillsides in the Mediterranean region; grown for its fruits.

Lookalikes

None.

Flowering and Fruiting Periods

Flowers July–August; fruit September–October.

The Olive tree is grown in the Mediterranean region for its fruit, and can successfully survive the heat and rocky hillsides of the area.

Gums

Evergreen, Large

Primary Features

Two kinds of leaves on the same tree – juvenile leaves, often blue and clasping the stem, sometimes green with short stalks; adult leaves long, drooping, lance-shaped.

Secondary Features

Medium-sized or large trees, often graceful. Flowers fluffy white clusters in the axils of the leaves. Flower buds form on the tree up to a year before they open.

Localities and Habits

Widely grown in parks and gardens and also commercially for their oil, timber and for paper.

Lookalikes

A large group of trees native to Australia of which about 12 are commonly grown in Europe, see p.345.

Flowering and Fruiting Periods

Flowers open in late summer.

Variety illustrated is Tasmanian Blue Gum

Tamarisk

Deciduous, Small

Primary Features

Leaves very small, scale-like, sheathing the twigs, giving the plant a feathery appearance.

Secondary Features

A shrub or small tree with very slender, graceful branches. Flowers pink or white in many dense clusters along the branches.

Localities and Habits

Often near the sea in southern Europe; planted and naturalized further north.

Lookalikes

None.

Flowering and Fruiting Periods

Flowers April–September; fruit July–October.

Oriental Plane

Deciduous, Large

Primary Features

Male catkins with 2–7 round, yellow heads; female catkins with 2–6 round, flattened heads, dark red when in full bloom.

Secondary Features

A large tree. Leaves five-lobed with the central lobe much longer than the others. Fruiting catkins with brownish-green heads and fine hooked spines on the seeds.

Localities and Habits

Widely planted in parks and gardens especially in southern Europe.

Lookalikes

London Plane p.194.

Flowering and Fruiting Periods

Flowering catkins April–June; fruit September–October.

London Plane

Deciduous, Large

Primary Features

Male catkins with 2–6 round yellow heads; female catkins with 2–5 round crimson heads.

Secondary Features

A large tree. Leaves five-lobed but the central lobe not longer than the rest. Fruiting catkins with brown heads and white hairs on the many seeds.

Localities and Habits

A tree very resistant to pollution and widely planted as a city street tree.

Lookalikes

Oriental Plane p.192.

Flowering and Fruiting Periods

Flowering catkins March–May; fruit September–October.

The London Plane is a pollution-resistant tree and therefore is widely used in cities.

Common Oak

Deciduous, Large

Primary Features

Fruits are acorns. Acorn cups relatively smooth, growing on stalks between 2–8 cm long, looking like a miniature smoker's pipe.

Secondary Features

A large broad tree. Leaves with 3–6 pairs of wavy-edged lobes and with small ear-like projections at the base. Male catkins yellow, in clusters, very slender. Female flowers terminal on new shoots, brownish, tiny.

Localities and Habits

Woodlands, hedgerows, mainly on heavy lime-rich soils throughout much of Europe except extreme north and south.

Lookalikes

Sessile Oak p.202; Turkey Oak p.204.

Flowering and Fruiting Periods

Flowers April–May; acorns ripen in September–October.

The distinctive lobe-edged leaves of the Common Oak are easy to spot, as are the fruits, the acorns with their cups.

Sessile or Durmast Oak

Deciduous, Large

Primary Features

Fruits are acorns. Acorn cups relatively smooth, with a very short stalk of less than 1 cm or stalkless.

Secondary Features

A large, domed tree. Leaves with 4–6 pairs of wavy-edged lobes and without small ear-like projections at the base. Male catkins greenish-yellow, in clusters, very slender. Female flowers tiny, whitish, in leaf axils.

Localities and Habits

Woodlands, hedgerows, mainly on acid, sandy soils throughout much of Europe except extreme north and south.

Lookalikes

Common Oak p.198; Turkey Oak p.204.

Flowering and Fruiting Periods

Flowers April–May; acorns ripen in September–October.

Turkey Oak

Deciduous, Large

Primary Features

Fruits are acorns. Acorn cups are stalkless, covered with long, curly, spreading scales.

Secondary Features

A large, domed tree with variable leaves. Leaves with 7–8 pairs of blunt lobes but without ear-like projections at the base. Male catkins red, in dense clusters, later brown. Female flowers tiny, yellow, in leaf axils.

Localities and Habits

Planted as a roadside and parkland tree in much of Europe. Native to the woodlands of southern Europe.

Lookalikes

Common Oak p.198; Sessile Oak p.202.

Flowering and Fruiting Periods

Flowers April–June; acorns ripen in September.

The Turkey Oak is native to southern Europe, and its leaves have more pointed lobes and more elaborate acorns than the Common Oak.

White Poplar

Deciduous, Large

Primary Features

Male catkins red and grey-fluffy; female catkins green at first, later fluffy with seed.

Secondary Features

A large spreading tree with many suckers. Young shoots and undersides of leaves with bright, white, furry down. Summer leaves of suckers always lobed, other leaves very variable in shape, basically rounded.

Localities and Habits

In wet woodland and on coasts, often spreading by suckers. Widely planted in much of Europe in gardens and streets.

Lookalikes

Grey Poplar p.110.

Flowering and Fruiting Periods

Catkins March–April, seeding in June.

The White Poplar boasts red male catkins, green female catkins and a white furry underside to the leaves.

Norway Maple

Deciduous, Large

Primary Features

Characteristic fruits in winged pairs have wings curving away from each other.

Secondary Features

A large spreading tree. Flowers greenish-yellow in large, broad, upright clusters of 30–40 flowers. Leaves large, with 5–7 pointed, toothed lobes; leaf-stalks red with milky juice.

Localities and Habits

Woodlands, hedgerows in much of Europe but only in uplands in southern Europe; an occasional street tree.

Lookalikes

Sycamore p.214; (Japanese Maple p.336).

Flowering and Fruiting Periods

Flowers March–April; fruit September–October.

Sycamore

Deciduous, Large

Primary Features

Characteristic fruits in winged pairs have wings curving towards each other.

Secondary Features

A large, spreading tree. Flowers yellow-green in large, drooping, narrow clusters of 60–100 flowers. Leaves with five, pointed, toothed lobes; leaf-stalks red without milky juice.

Localities and Habits

Woodlands, hedgerows in much of Europe; extensively introduced and naturalized; a common street tree.

Lookalikes

Norway Maple p.212; (Japanese Maple p.336).

Flowering and Fruiting Periods

Flowers April–June; fruit September–October.

The winged fruit of the Sycamore looks similar to that of the Norway Maple, but the wings of each pair curve towards each other, rather than away.

Field Maple

Deciduous, Small

Primary Features

Characteristic fruits in winged pairs with wings spreading horizontally, often tinged with red.

Secondary Features

A shrub or small tree. Flowers pale green in small, upright clusters of 10–20 flowers. Leaves small, with 3–5 rounded lobes; leaf-stalks red with milky juice.

Localities and Habits

Hedgerows, woodland and scrub on lime-rich soils especially in northern areas of Europe.

Lookalikes

(Montpelier Maple p.336).

Flowering and Fruiting Periods

Flowers April–May; fruit September–October.

The Field Maple is suited best to the lime-rich soils of northern Europe, where it thrives.

Hawthorn or May

Deciduous, Small

Primary Features

Fruits are large clusters of round, deep-red, single-stoned berries developing from similar clusters of white, pink-tinged, heavily scented flowers.

Secondary Features

A large, dense, thorny shrub or small tree. Leaves with 3–7 deep rounded lobes, green and mostly hairless on both surfaces.

Localities and Habits

Very common in woodland, hedgerows and scrubland throughout Europe.

Lookalikes

(Midland Hawthorn p.337).

Flowering and Fruiting Periods

Flowers March–June; fruit August–November.

The thorny branches of the Hawthorn or May tree have clusters of white blossom, later followed by deep-red berries.

Swedish Whitebeam

Deciduous, Small

Primary Features

Fruits are large clusters of oblong, red-brown berries developing from similar clusters of white flowers in which the flower-stalks are covered with grey down.

Secondary Features

A shrub or small tree. Leaves longer than broad with 6–8 pairs of small lobes, grey-woolly beneath, especially when young.

Localities and Habits

A northern European species, often planted as a street tree in more southern areas.

Lookalikes

Whitebeam p.102; Wild Service Tree p.228.

Flowering and Fruiting Periods

Flowers May; fruit September.

Wild Service Tree

Deciduous, Medium

Primary Features

Fruits are clusters of long, brown berries developing from similar clusters of white flowers in which the flower-stalks are woolly.

Secondary Features

A medium-sized, spreading tree. Leaves broader than long, with 3–4 pairs of triangular, toothed lobes, green on both sides, somewhat woolly below.

Localities and Habits

Woodlands, scattered throughout much of Europe.

Lookalikes

(Service Tree of Fontainebleau p.337); Norway Maple p.212; Sycamore p.214.

Flowering and Fruiting Periods

Flowers May–June; fruit September.

Fig

Deciduous, Small

Primary Features

Fruits large, succulent, pear-shaped, solitary and green.

Secondary Features

A shrub or small tree, often trained against a wall. Twigs with milky juice. Leaves dark green, leathery or rough, with 3–7 deep, rounded lobes. Male and female flowers in separate flask-shaped receptacles.

Localities and Habits

Cultivated for its fruit throughout southern Europe; also grows in more northern areas.

Lookalikes

None.

Flowering and Fruiting Periods

Flowers June–September; fruit July–October.

Tree of Heaven

Deciduous, Medium

Primary Features

Large, hanging clusters of winged fruits, usually brown, sometimes reddish, each with a seed at the centre of the twisted wing.

Secondary Features

A medium-sized tree. Leaves up to 1 m long with 13–41 leaflets, each one with a red stalk and 2–4 teeth near the base. Flowers unpleasantly scented, greenish, in large clusters at the ends of the shoots.

Localities and Habits

Grown as a street tree and in parks throughout Europe.

Lookalikes

None.

Flowering and Fruiting Periods

Flowers July–August; fruit August–September.

Common Ash

Deciduous, Medium

Primary Features

Large, hanging clusters of winged fruits, at first green later brown; each 2–5.5 cm long with a seed at the base of the wing.

Secondary Features

A medium-sized tree. Leaves opposite, up to 30 cm long with 7–13 leaflets. Flowers petalless, purple clusters appearing before the leaves which open in early summer.

Localities and Habits

Woodland especially on lime-rich soils, throughout Europe.

Lookalikes

Manna Ash p.238; (Narrow-Leaved Ash p.337).

Flowering and Fruiting Periods

Flowers April–May; fruit October–November.

The Common Ash is widespread in Britain, growing in places where flowing water is abundant. It can reach up to 24 m tall, more in favourable conditions.

Manna Ash

Deciduous, Small

Primary Features

Large, hanging clusters of winged fruits, at first green, later brown, each 1.5–2.5 cm long with a seed at the base of the wing.

Secondary Features

A small tree. Leaves opposite, up to 30 cm long, with 5–9 leaflets. Flowers with creamy-white, scented petals appearing with the leaves in pyramidal clusters.

Localities and Habits

Native to the Mediterranean region in woods and thickets; also planted in parks and gardens in more northern areas.

Lookalikes

Common Ash p.234; (Narrow-Leaved Ash p.337).

Flowering and Fruiting Periods

Flowers April–May; fruit July–September.

Walnut

Deciduous, Large

Primary Features

Round, smooth, green fruits enclose the wrinkled stones. The seeds are edible nuts.

Secondary Features

A large spreading tree. Leaves up to 45 cm long, with 3–9 (usually 7) leaflets; basal leaflets smaller than terminal ones. Male catkins yellow, drooping; female flowers small, green; both on young shoots.

Localities and Habits

Planted and naturalized throughout much of Europe.

Lookalikes

None.

Flowering and Fruiting Periods

Flowers May–June; fruit September–October.

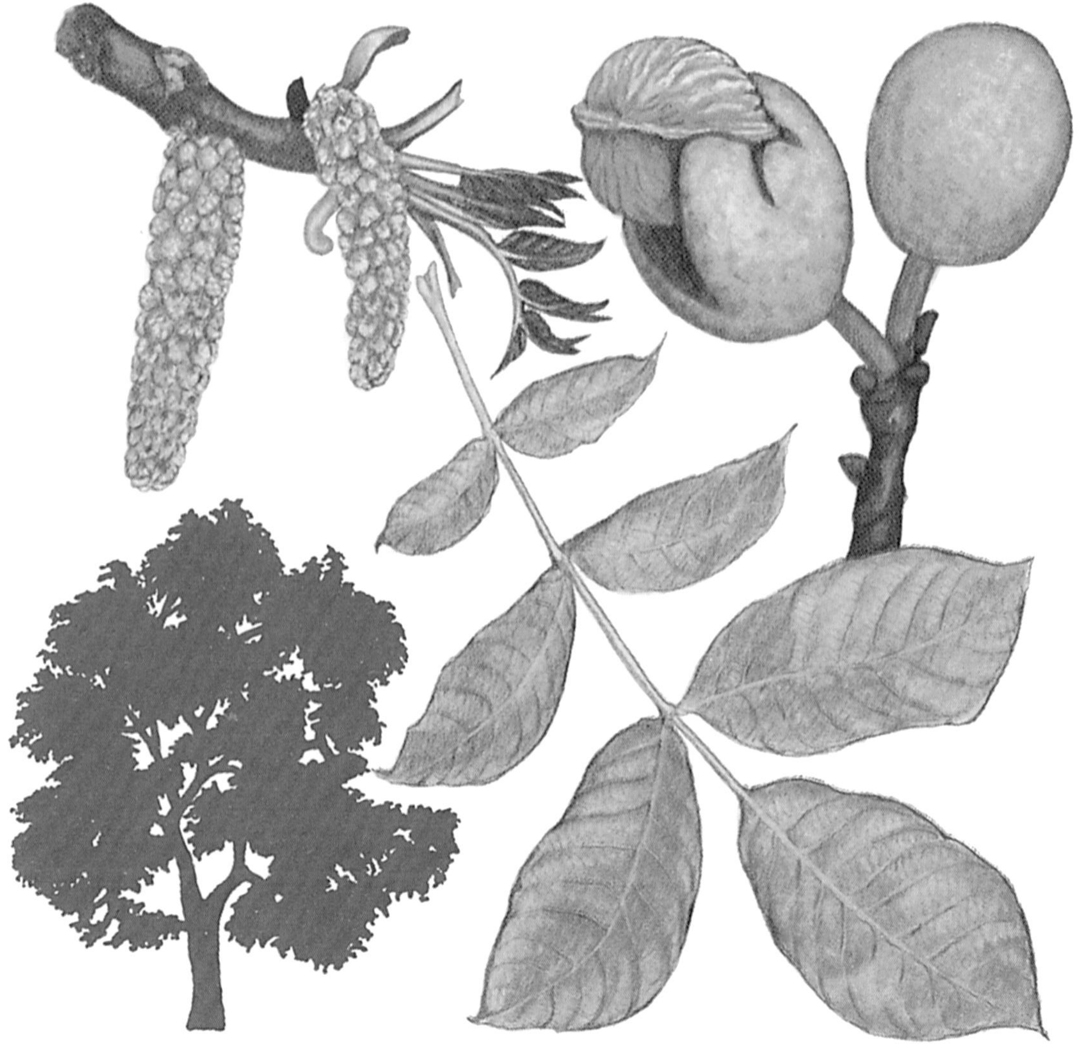

The seeds of the Walnut tree are enclosed in round green fruit, and are in fact the edible nuts – walnuts.

Horse Chestnut

Deciduous, Large

Primary Features

Round, green, softly spiny fruits enclose 1–3 brown, shiny seeds – the horse chestnuts or 'conkers'.

Secondary Features

A large spreading tree. Leaves with 5–7 leaflets, all growing from the same point and with long leaf-stalks. Flowers white or pink in large, showy pyramidal clusters.

Localities and Habits

Extensively planted and naturalized in towns and cities throughout much of Europe; a common street tree.

Lookalikes

(Red Horse Chestnut p.337).

Flowering and Fruiting Periods

Flowers April–May; fruit September.

Service Tree

Deciduous, Medium

Primary Features

Fruit a small cluster of green or brown pear-shaped berries with gritty flesh.

Secondary Features

A medium-sized tree with a domed crown. Leaves with 13–21 toothed leaflets, up to 22 cm long. Flowers with five separate, creamy-white petals, in large clusters; flower-stalks downy.

Localities and Habits

Planted as an ornamental tree and naturalized throughout much of Europe; also grown for its fruit.

Lookalikes

Rowan p.250.

Flowering and Fruiting Periods

Flowers May; fruit July–August.

The Service Tree is an ornamental tree with clusters of green or brown pear-shaped berries, which are edible.

Rowan or Mountain Ash

Deciduous, Small

Primary Features

Large clusters of berries, at first yellow turning orange then quickly red to be devoured by the birds.

Secondary Features

A small- or medium-sized tree. Leaves with 9–19 toothed leaflets, up to 25 cm long. Flowers with five separate, creamy-white petals and downy flower-stalks, in large clusters.

Localities and Habits

Hedgerows and hillsides over much of Europe; often planted as a street tree.

Lookalikes

Service Tree p.246.

Flowering and Fruiting Periods

Flowers May; fruit July (yellow) – September (red).

The Rowan or Mountain Ash is a popular tree in many countries of Europe, and the birds enjoy it too, devouring the berries that first appear in July.

Elder

Deciduous, Small

Primary Features

Fruit a heavy, flat-topped cluster of round, black, juicy berries.

Secondary Features

A shrub or small tree often with arching branches. Leaves opposite, with 3–9 toothed leaflets. Flowers white, scented, tubular, in large flat-topped clusters; flower-stalks not downy.

Localities and Habits

Damp woodland, waste places and hedgerows throughout much of Europe.

Lookalikes

None.

Flowering and Fruiting Periods

Flowers June–July; fruit August–November.

Both the clusters of flowers and the berries of the Elder tree can be used for culinary purposes – cordial and jelly, for instance.

Laburnum

Deciduous, Small

Primary Features

Flowers bright yellow, pea-like, in long, loose, drooping chains.

Secondary Features

A small tree. Leaves with three leaflets. Fruits like pea-pods, green and hairy when young, dry and brown when mature; up to 10 black seeds in each pod. The whole plant is very poisonous.

Localities and Habits

Woods and scrub in southern Europe. Widely planted in streets and gardens throughout much of Europe.

Lookalikes

(Scotch Laburnum p.337).

Flowering and Fruiting Periods

Flowers May–June; fruit July–August.

Despite being widely planted in streets and gardens, the whole of the Laburnum plant is very poisonous.

Locust Tree

Deciduous, Medium

Primary Features

Flowers white, sweet-scented, like sweet peas in drooping clusters.

Secondary Features

A medium-sized tree, often with many suckers. Leaves up to 20 cm long with 13–15 leaflets, yellowish in colour and often with a spine at the base. Fruits are like clusters of brown pea-pods.

Localities and Habits

Hedgerows, parks and gardens especially in western and southern Europe on sandy soils.

Lookalikes

None.

Flowering and Fruiting Periods

Flowers June; fruit October.

Mimosa

Deciduous, Medium

Primary Features

Flowers bright yellow, fragrant balls in long, drooping chains.

Secondary Features

A medium-sized tree. Leaves up to 12 cm long with 13–25 pairs of feathery leaflets, silvery grey or yellowish-green in colour. Fruits are like flattened pea-pods.

Localities and Habits

Introduced and widely planted in southern Europe for ornament and to stabilize sandy soils and dunes.

Lookalikes

None.

Flowering and Fruiting Periods

Flowers January–February; fruit May.

Cabbage Palm

Evergreen, Small

Primary Features

Leaves lance-shaped, up to 90 cm long, sharp-pointed, dark green and fibrous.

Secondary Features

A palm-like tree with several 'trunks' and suckers, each with a dense crown of leaves. Flowers creamy white and fragrant, in large spikes over 1 m tall. Fruits are bluish-white berries.

Localities and Habits

Streets, parks and gardens in coastal areas of southern and western Europe.

Lookalikes

None.

Flowering and Fruiting Periods

Flowers in spring (native climes).

The creamy-white flower spikes of the Cabbage Palm can measure over 1 m long and are followed by bluish-white berries.

Chusan Palm

Evergreen, Small

Primary Features

Leaves up to 1 m in diameter, fan-shaped, divided into 50–60 stiff, pointed lobes and with leaf-stalks covered with long, brown fibres.

Secondary Features

A medium-sized tree with a crown of leaves growing from the top of the trunk and with dead leaves partly covering the trunk. Flowers yellow, fragrant, growing in a large spike. Fruits like purple berries.

Localities and Habits

The most hardy and most widely planted of all the palms; only flowering in more southern areas.

Lookalikes

Dwarf Fan Palm p.272.

Flowering and Fruiting Periods

Flowers and fruits; continuous in tropical climate.

Dwarf Fan Palm

Evergreen, Small

Primary Features

Leaves up to 1 m in diameter, fan-shaped, divided into 12–20 stiff, lance-shaped leaflets. Leaf-stalks armed with sharp spines.

Secondary Features

A dwarf palm with a short trunk and many suckers, forming a dense clump. Flowers yellow, often hidden, in large dense clusters. Fruits brown inedible berries.

Localities and Habits

The only native European palm, growing on sandy coastlines in the western Mediterranean.

Lookalikes

Chusan Palm p.270.

Flowering and Fruiting Periods

Flowers and fruits; continuous in tropical climate.

Canary Island Date Palm

Evergreen, Medium

Primary Features

Leaves 5–6 m long, compound, with 100–200 pairs of spiny leaflets in a dense crown of up to 200 leaves at the top of stout 'trunk'.

Secondary Features

A medium-sized tree. Flowers in large clusters in the axils of the leaves developing into large clusters of smooth, brown fruits with dry, tasteless flesh.

Localities and Habits

Frequently planted as a street tree and in gardens in southern Europe.

Lookalikes

None.

Flowering and Fruiting Periods

Flowers and fruits; continuous in tropical climate.

Yew

Evergreen, Medium

Primary Features

Fruit is a fleshy, oval berry, bright red in colour, about 1 cm long and containing one seed.

Secondary Features

Eventually a medium-sized tree with a huge trunk. Leaves 1–3 cm long, very dark green above, lighter green below and with a short stalk, arranged in two rows. Male flowers in cones. Seeds and leaves poisonous.

Localities and Habits

Woodlands and scrub on lime-rich soils in much of Europe; often planted as a hedge or in churchyards.

Lookalikes

There are many cultivated varieties, differing mainly in their form and in the colour of their leaves, see p.346.

Flowering and Fruiting Periods

Flowering cones March–April; fruit August–September.

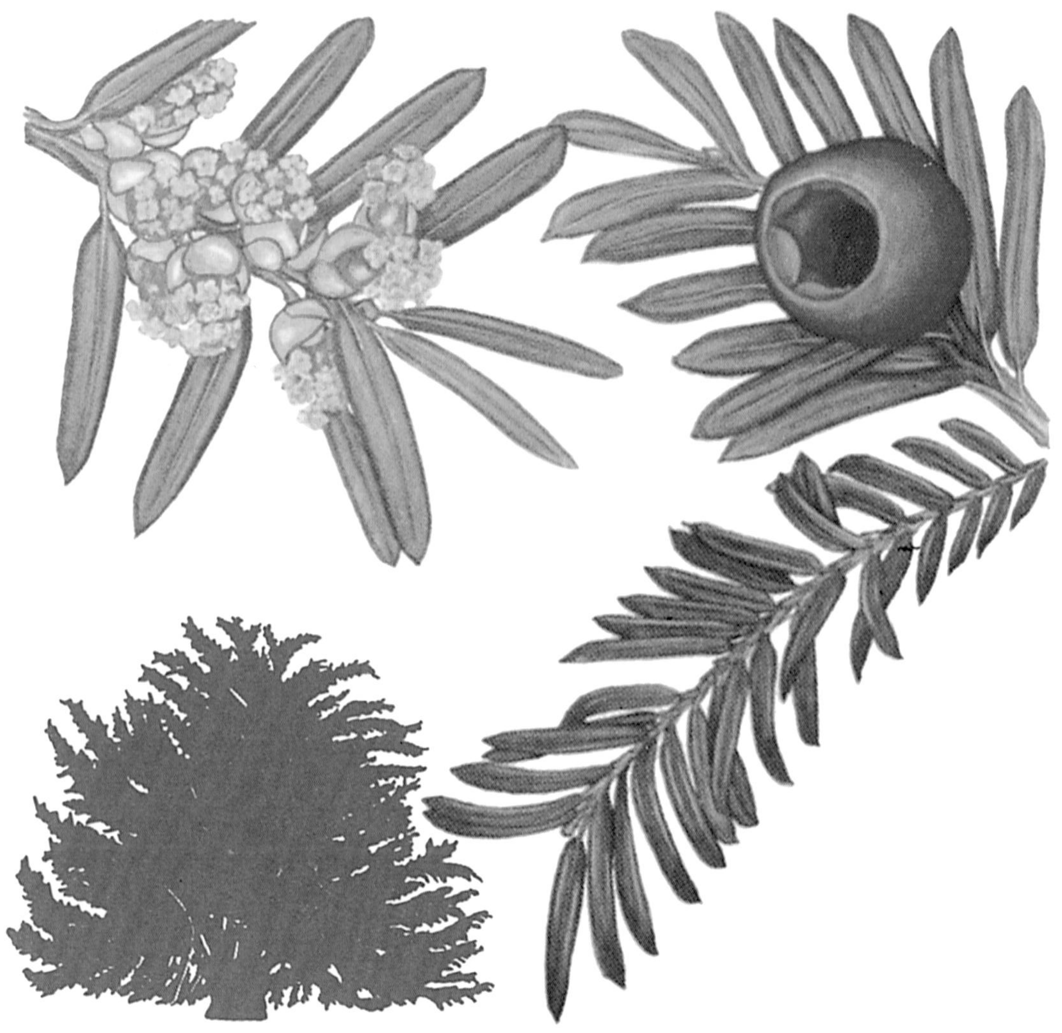

Douglas Fir

Evergreen, Large

Primary Features

Leaves soft, 2–2.5 cm long, dark green above with two whitish bands below; spreading in two complex rows along each side of the branches.

Secondary Features

A very tall conical tree. Leaf scars slightly prominent. Female cones drooping, green at first, brown when mature, 5–10 cm long with prominent spiky, brown bracts. Cones shed whole.

Localities and Habits

Introduced and planted for timber in much of Europe.

Lookalikes

Silver Fir p.282; Noble Fir p.284; (Western Hemlock p.339).

Flowering and Fruiting Periods

Flowering cones: March–April.

The Douglas Fir serves as a widespread timber source in much of Europe and grows to a great height.

Silver Fir

Evergreen, Large

Primary Features

Leaves 1–2 cm long, shining green above, silvery below, arranged in four rows along the branches when viewed from above.

Secondary Features

A tall pyramidal tree. Leaves make flat round scars on the twigs when they fall off. Female cones erect, in clusters near top of tree, green at first, mature cones brown, 10–14 cm long, breaking up on tree to release seeds.

Localities and Habits

Forms mountain forests in central and southern Europe. Planted for timber throughout much of Europe.

Lookalikes

Noble Fir p.284; (Spanish Fir p.338); Douglas Fir p.278.

Flowering and Fruiting Periods

Flowering cones: April.

Noble Fir

Evergreen, Large

Primary Features

Leaves 1.5–3.5 cm long, leathery, strongly curved, blue-green on both sides; curving around the branches from below, in four rows.

Secondary Features

A very tall conical tree. Leaves make flat round scars on twigs when they fall off. Female cones erect, yellowish at first, purple-brown with green bracts when mature, up to 25 cm long, breaking up on tree to release seeds.

Localities and Habits

Introduced and planted for timber in northern and western Europe; also for ornament in parks and gardens.

Lookalikes

(Giant Fir p.338); Silver Fir p.282; Douglas Fir p.278.

Flowering and Fruiting Periods

Flowering cones: April–May.

Norway Spruce

Evergreen, Large

Primary Features

Leaves hard, green, 1–2 cm long with pointed tips, spirally arranged on branches, not in rows.

Secondary Features

A tall conical tree. Leaves make peg-like projections on twigs when they fall off. Female cones erect and green at first, maturing brown and drooping, 10–15 cm long, growing near the top of the tree, shed whole.

Localities and Habits

Upland areas in much of Europe; also planted in parks or for timber; young ones are used as Christmas trees.

Lookalikes

Serbian Spruce p.288; (Sitka Spruce p.338); (Oriental Spruce p.338); (Blue Spruce p.338).

Flowering and Fruiting Periods

Flowering cones: May–June.

Serbian Spruce

Evergreen, Large

Primary Features

Leaves flattened, 1–2 cm long with blunt tips, green above with two white bands below; spirally arranged on branches, not in rows.

Secondary Features

A tall conical tree. Leaves make peg-like projections on twigs when they fall off. Female cones drooping from topmost branches, red at first, maturing dark brown, 3–6 cm long, shed whole.

Localities and Habits

Planted in northern Europe for timber; also in city parks and gardens since it is resistant to pollution.

Lookalikes

Norway Spruce p.286; (Sitka Spruce p.338); (Oriental Spruce p.338); (Blue Spruce p.338).

Flowering and Fruiting Periods

Flowering cones: May.

European Larch

Deciduous, Large

Primary Features

Leaves 1–3 cm long, growing in clusters of 30–40, very bright green especially in spring when new leaves appear.

Secondary Features

A tall conical tree. Female cones have conspicuous red bracts when young, maturing into egg-shaped, brown cones, 2–3.5 cm long, which remain on tree after the seeds are shed.

Localities and Habits

Planted for timber and in parks and gardens in much of Europe; often naturalized.

Lookalikes

Japanese Larch p.294.

Flowering and Fruiting Periods

Flowering cones: March–April.

The egg-shaped cones of the European Larch remain on the tree even after the seeds have been shed.

Japanese Larch

Deciduous, Large

Primary Features

Leaves 1.5–3.5 cm long, growing in clusters of about 40, bluish-green with two white bands on the lower surface.

Secondary Features

A broad conical tree. Female cones have rather inconspicuous greenish bracts when young, maturing into rounded, egg-shaped, brown cones, 1.5–3.5 cm long, remaining on the tree after the seeds are shed.

Localities and Habits

Planted for timber in northern and western areas of Europe.

Lookalikes

European Larch p.290.

Flowering and Fruiting Periods

Flowering cones: March–April.

Cedar of Lebanon

Evergreen, Large

Primary Features

Leaves 2–3 cm long, growing in clusters of 10–15, blue-green to dark green; young shoots grow horizontally.

Secondary Features

A large tree with ascending branches forming a flat-topped, spreading crown. Male and female cones both large, upright and conspicuous, male cones grey-green, female cones brown, breaking up on tree to release seeds.

Localities and Habits

Pollution-tolerant species from the Middle East; widely planted in parks and churchyards.

Lookalikes

Deodar Cedar p.298; (Atlas Cedar p.339).

Flowering and Fruiting Periods

Flowering cones: October–February.

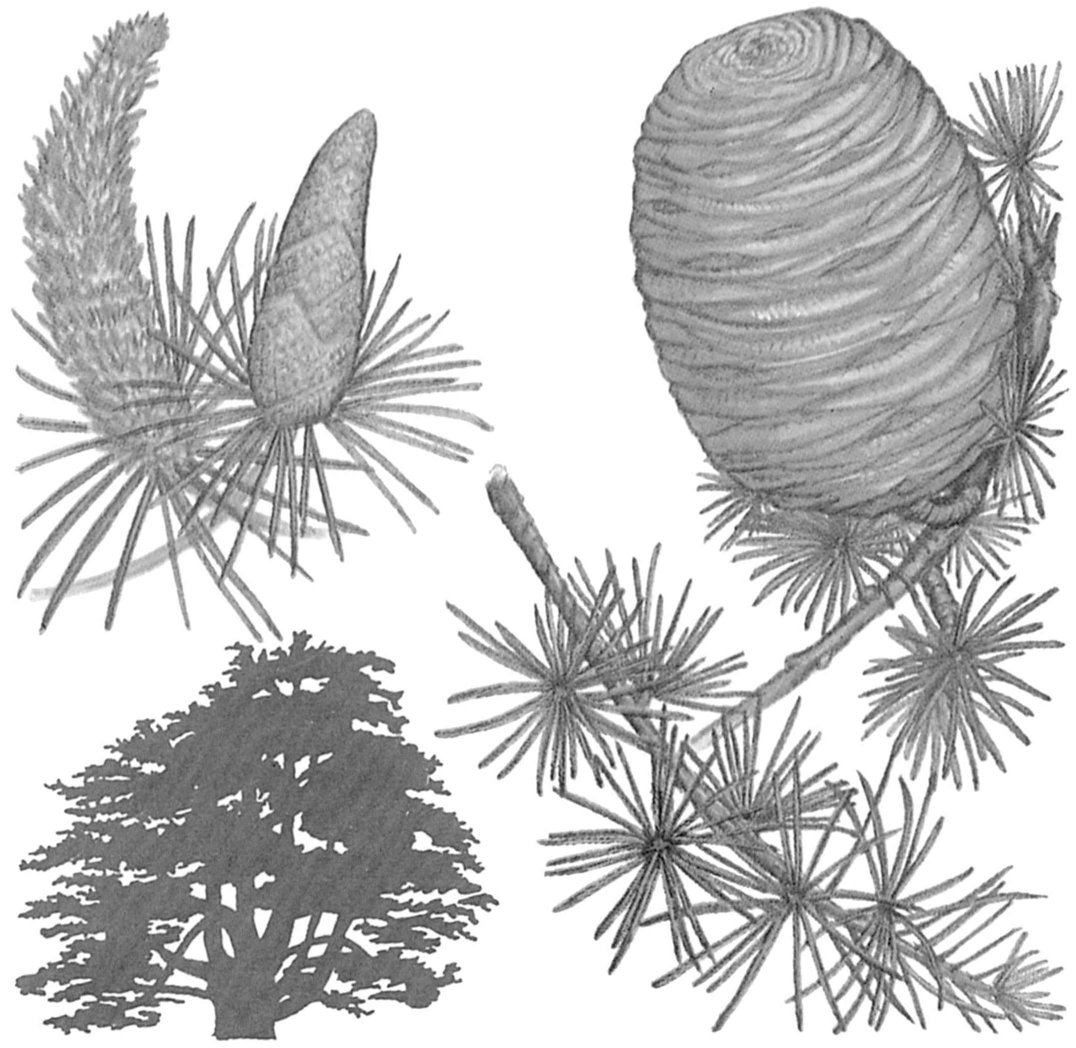

Deodar Cedar

Evergreen, Large

Primary Features

Leaves 2–5 cm long, growing in clusters of 15–20, dark green or yellowish-green; young shoots arching downwards.

Secondary Features

Young trees with weeping branches, mature trees broadly conical. Male and female cones both large, upright, conspicuous; male cones purple, female cones brown, breaking up on tree to release seeds.

Localities and Habits

Widely planted in parks and gardens throughout much of Europe and for timber in southern areas.

Lookalikes

Cedar of Lebanon p.296; (Atlas Cedar p.339).

Flowering and Fruiting Periods

Flowering cones: November.

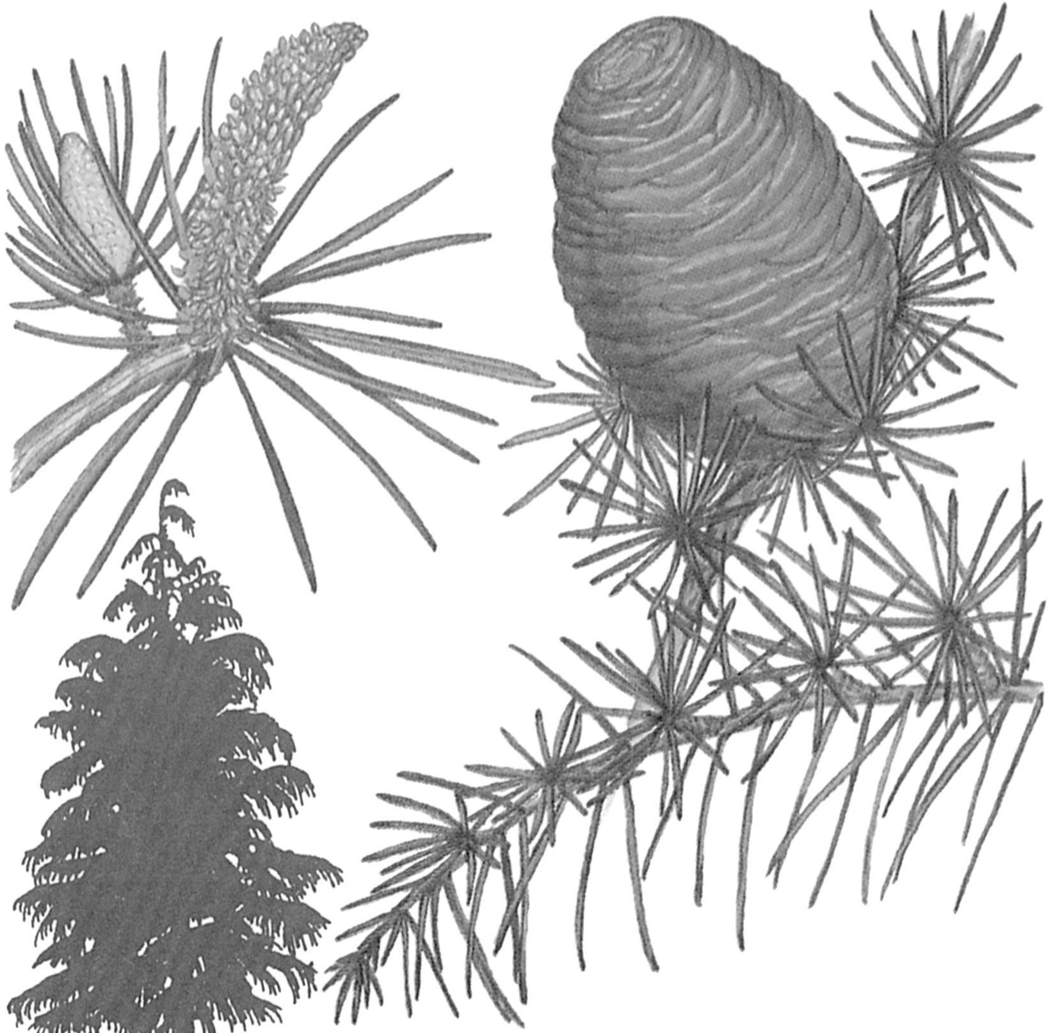

Maritime Pine

Evergreen, Medium

Primary Features

Leaves 10–20 cm long, growing in pairs, very thick and rigid, whitish-green, not particularly dense on the branches.

Secondary Features

A medium-sized tree with widely spaced branches at the top. Mature females cones 8–22 cm long, light shining brown, stalkless, remaining on tree after seeds are shed.

Localities and Habits

Light soils and dunes in the Mediterranean region; now grown in similar areas further north.

Lookalikes

Scots Pine p.304; Austrian Pine p.302; (Monterey Pine p.339); (Stone Pine p.339).

Flowering and Fruiting Periods

Flowering cones: May–June.

Austrian Pine

Evergreen, Large

Primary Features

Leaves 10–15 cm long, growing in pairs and very densely clothing the branches, very dark green, stiff, straight or twisted.

Secondary Features

A tall tree with a crown of branches at the top. Mature female cones 5–8 cm long, yellow-brown, almost stalkless, remaining on tree after seeds are shed.

Localities and Habits

Planted in shelter belts especially in coastal areas and on chalky soils in much of Europe.

Lookalikes

(Corsican Pine p.340); Scots Pine p.304; Maritime Pine p.300; (Aleppo Pine p.340).

Flowering and Fruiting Periods

Flowering cones: May–June.

Scots Pine

Evergreen, Large

Primary Features

Leaves 3–10 cm long, blue-green and twisted, growing in pairs and sparsely clothing the branches.

Secondary Features

A medium-sized to tall tree with a crown of branches at the top. Mature female cones 2–8 cm long, grey-brown, on short stalks, remaining on tree after seeds are shed.

Localities and Habits

Most widely distributed of all the pines in Europe, growing on light sandy soils, especially in upland areas.

Lookalikes

Austrian Pine p.302; Maritime Pine p.300; (Stone Pine p.339).

Flowering and Fruiting Periods

Flowering cones: May–June.

Arolla Pine

Evergreen, Large

Primary Features

Leaves 5–8 cm long, stiff, dark green above and whitish below, growing in clusters of five and very densely clothing the branches.

Secondary Features

A pyramidal tree with branches almost to the ground. Young shoots covered in distinctive orange-brown fur. Mature female cones purplish-brown, on short stalks, about 8 cm long, shed whole.

Localities and Habits

Native to the Alps and Carpathian Mountains and also planted for timber in other areas of Europe.

Lookalikes

(Bhutan Pine p.340); (Weymouth Pine p.340).

Flowering and Fruiting Periods

Flowering cones: May–June.

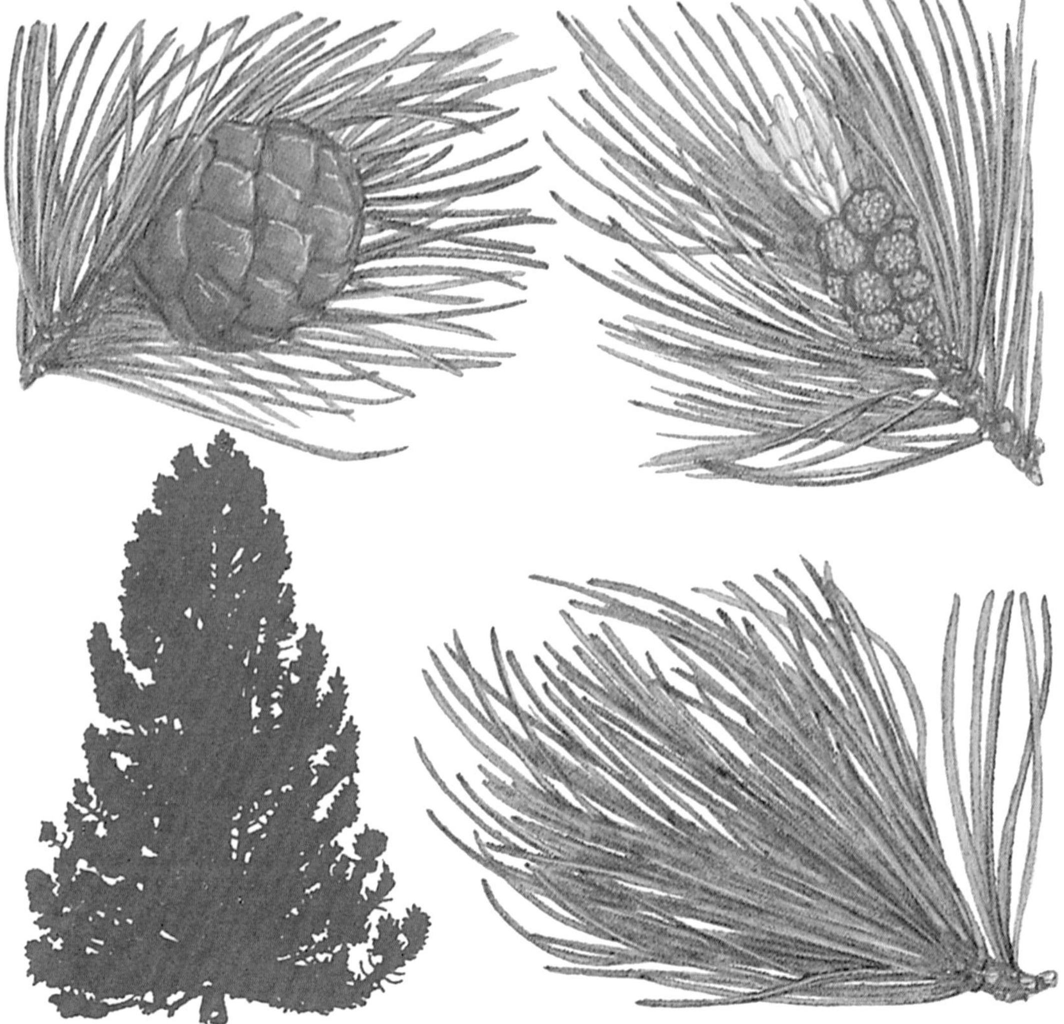

Common Juniper

Evergreen, Small

Primary Features

Fruit a green berry, changing to blue-black when ripening after a year on the plant, containing several seeds.

Secondary Features

A spreading shrub or small tree. Leaves small, rigid and pointed, in whorls of three, dark green below with a white stripe above. Male flowers in cones on separate trees from the female cones.

Localities and Habits

Chalk or limestone downlands and acid heathlands throughout Europe.

Lookalikes

There are many cultivated varieties. (Prickly Juniper p.340); Chinese Juniper p.312.

Flowering and Fruiting Periods

Flowering cones: May–June; fruit September–October.

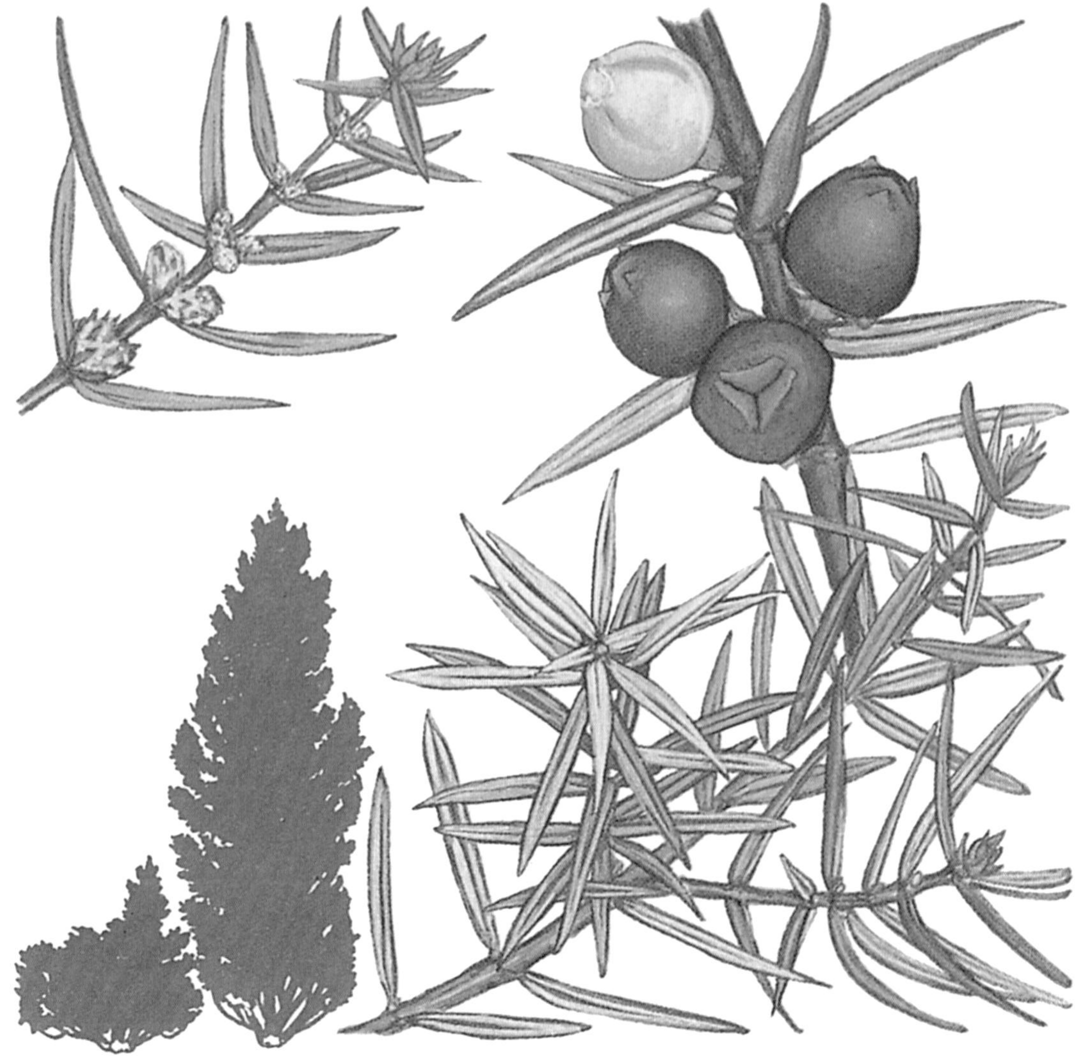

The small, rigid pointed leaves of the Common Juniper are evergreen. The berries take a year to ripen from green to black on the shrub.

Chinese Juniper

Evergreen, Small

Primary Features

Fruit a bluish-white berry, changing to purplish-brown when ripening after a year on the plant; containing several seeds.

Secondary Features

A small conical tree. It has two kinds of leaves – juvenile, prickly, blue-green needles and adult, scale-like, dark-green leaves closely pressed to the stems. Male and female flowering cones on separate trees.

Localities and Habits

Planted in parks, gardens and churchyards throughout much of Europe.

Lookalikes

Common Juniper p.308; (Pencil Juniper p.341); (Phoenician Juniper p.341); ('Skyrocket' p.346).

Flowering and Fruiting Periods

Flowering cones: March–April; fruit takes two years to ripen.

Monkey Puzzle Tree

Evergreen, Large

Primary Features

Very distinctive appearance with thick, regularly arranged, horizontal or drooping branches clothed with large, thick, glossy-green leaves.

Secondary Features

A large, domed tree. Male and female cones on separate trees. Mature female cones round, brown, upright on upper sides of branches, breaking up on tree to release seeds. Male cones brown, in clusters, at tips of branches.

Localities and Habits

Introduced and planted in parks and gardens especially in western Europe.

Lookalikes

None.

Flowering and Fruiting Periods

Flowering cones: July.

Western Red Cedar

Evergreen, Large

Primary Features

Female cones numerous, conical in shape, about 1 cm long, leathery, green at first, later brown; only middle three scales bear seeds, 2–3 on each scale.

Secondary Features

A large pyramidal tree with an erect leading tip and feathery foliage which smells of pear-drops. Leaves opposite, green above, whitish beneath. Male cones minute, almost invisible on tips of shoots.

Localities and Habits

Introduced and widely planted for timber and as a hedge throughout Europe.

Lookalikes

Lawson Cypress p.320; Leyland Cypress p.322; (White Cedar p.341); ('Zebrina' p.346).

Flowering and Fruiting Periods

Flowering cones: March.

The Western Red Cedar is a large tree with a pear-drop scent, and is a source of European timber.

Lawson Cypress

Evergreen, Large

Primary Features

Female cones numerous, round, about 8 mm in diameter, green at first, later brown and woody with all eight scales bearing seeds, 2–5 on each side.

Secondary Features

A large conical tree with a drooping leading tip and feathery foliage with a distinctive resinous scent. Leaves opposite, dark green above, whitish beneath. Male cones up to 5 mm in diameter on tips of shoots.

Localities and Habits

Introduced and widely planted for timber and as a hedge throughout Europe.

Lookalikes

There are many cultivated varieties, differing mainly in their size and shape, see p.346–47. Leyland Cypress p.322.

Flowering and Fruiting Periods

Flowering cones: February–April.

Leyland Cypress

Evergreen, Large

Primary Features

Male and female cones rare. Female cones, when produced, are round, brown and shiny, 2–3 cm in diameter with 4–8 scales, usually seedless.

Secondary Features

A large conical tree with a leaning leading tip and feathery foliage with a resinous scent. Leaves opposite, green above, yellowish below.

Localities and Habits

Extensively planted as a hedging plant throughout much of Europe.

Lookalikes

There are several cultivated varieties, differing mainly in the colour of their leaves, see p.346–47.

Lawson Cypress p.320.

Flowering and Fruiting Periods

Flowering cones: March.

Monterey Cypress

Evergreen, Medium

Primary Features

Female cones numerous, round and lumpy, about 3 cm in diameter; green at first, later purple-brown and shiny; all eight scales bear seeds, 8–20 on each scale.

Secondary Features

A medium-sized domed tree with an erect leading tip and feathery, lemon-scented foliage. Leaves opposite, deep green. Male cones about 3 mm in diameter on tips of shoots behind female cones.

Localities and Habits

Introduced and planted in southern and western Europe especially as a hedge plant.

Lookalikes

There are several cultivated varieties, see p.346–47. Italian Cypress p.326; Leyland Cypress p.322.

Flowering and Fruiting Periods

Flowering cones: March.

Italian Cypress

Evergreen, Medium

Primary Features

This form of the Italian Cypress is a very narrow tree with ascending branches and ascending, feathery shoots with dark-green, opposite leaves.

Secondary Features

Female cones numerous, round, 2–4 cm in diameter, green at first, later dull yellowish-grey, with 8–14 scales all bearing 8–20 seeds. Males cones about 4 mm in diameter on tips of shoots.

Localities and Habits

Widely planted in Europe especially in the Mediterranean region where its upright form makes it conspicuous.

Lookalikes

There is also a columnar form of this tree, p.341; Monterey Cypress p.324.

Flowering and Fruiting Periods

Flowering cones: March.

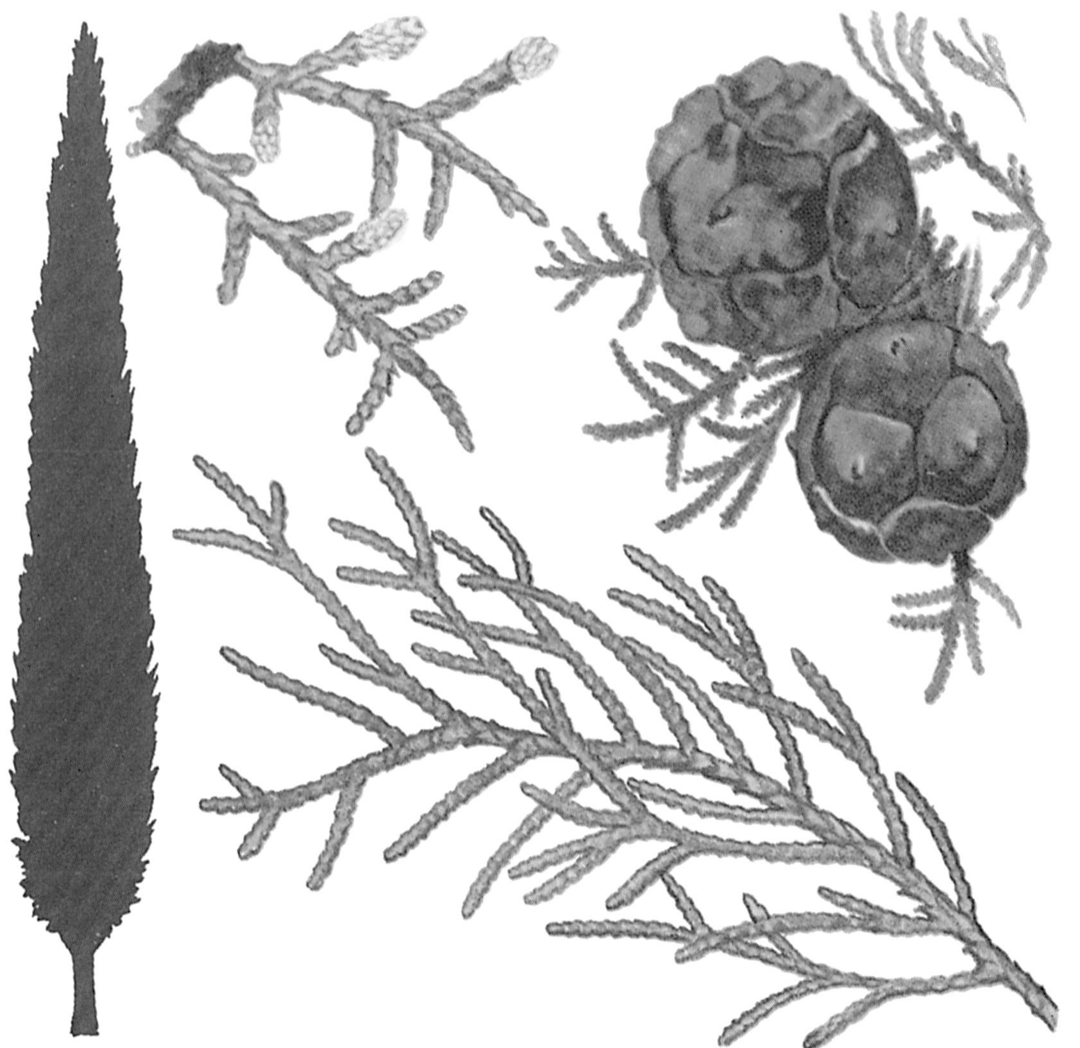

The ascending branches and shoots of the Italian Cypress help to form its very narrow shape, which is particularly popular in the Mediterranean region.

Lookalikes and Cultivars

Almond Willow (1)
A shrub. Leaves hairless, 3–8 times as long as broad.

Chinese Weeping Willow (2)
Long weeping branches have brown bark.

Peach (3)
Flowers deep pink; fruits velvety yellow-red peaches.

Rum Cherry (4)
A large tree. Leaves have orange hairs on undersides.

Japanese Spindle Tree (5)
A small evergreen tree most often found in southern Europe.

Lookalikes and Cultivars

Sour Cherry (6)
A shrub with red cherries – the Morello cherry.

Grey Willow (7)
A shrub with slender catkins and narrow leaves.

Black Poplar (8)
A large tree with black bark and bosses on trunk.

Black Italian Poplar (9)
A large tree with black bark but no bosses.

Japonica (10)
Flowers scarlet in small clusters on old wood.

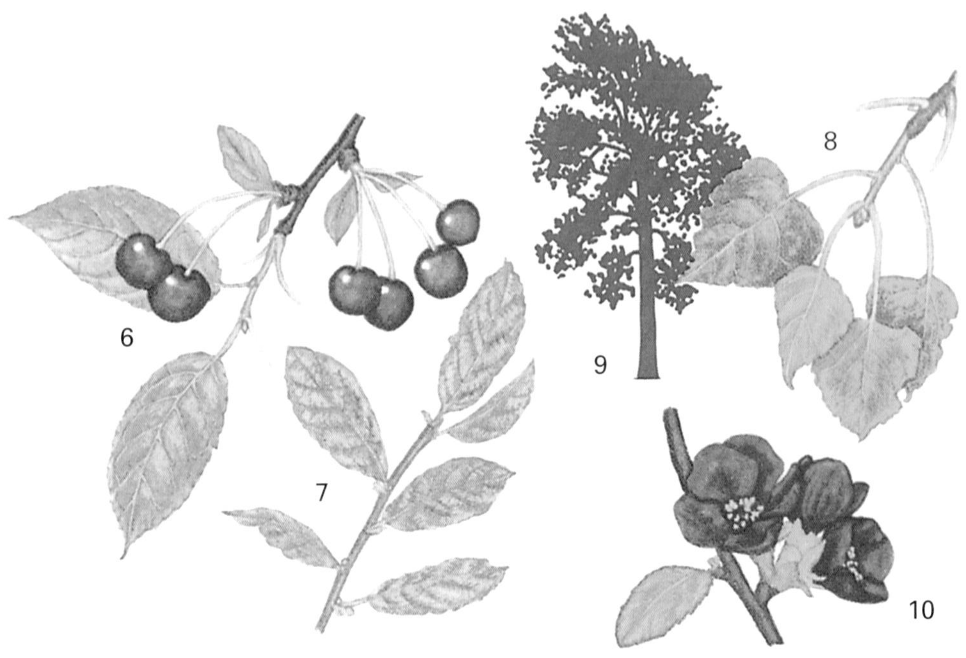

The Black Poplar is a large deciduous tree that is unfortunately in decline in England because its habitat is disappearing to make way for urban development.